The Great Ninja
CREAMi
Cookbook 2023

Enjoy 1800 Days of Simple and Mouthwatering Homemade Frozen Treats | Ice Creams, Sorbets, tasty Ice Cream Mix-Ins, Smoothies & Shakes

Marwan R. Ghabour

Table of Contents

Chapter 6 Milkshake Recipes 44

INTRODUCTION

Welcome to the world of frozen desserts! As a professional chef in the United States, I am excited to introduce you to a new and innovative way of creating delicious, homemade frozen treats with the Ninja Creami ice cream maker. This cookbook is designed to provide you with a collection of mouth-watering recipes that are easy to follow and will help you unleash your inner creativity in the kitchen.

The Ninja Creami is a state-of-the-art kitchen appliance that has revolutionized the way we make ice cream, sorbet, gelato, and other frozen desserts. With its powerful motor and freezing bowl, the Ninja Creami makes it possible to whip up a batch of homemade ice cream in just a few minutes, without the need for expensive equipment or lengthy preparation times.

All about Your Appliance

The Ninja Creami is a modern kitchen appliance designed to simplify the process of making homemade frozen desserts. This innovative appliance combines a powerful motor with a freezing bowl to create a fast and efficient system for churning and freezing dessert mixtures.

The Ninja Creami's freezing bowl is an essential component of the machine. It must be pre-frozen in a standard freezer for at least 24 hours before use, ensuring that it is at the appropriate temperature to freeze the dessert mixture efficiently. Once the bowl is frozen, the user can add their desired ingredients and turn on the machine. The motor drives a blade that churns and freezes the mixture, producing a creamy, smooth consistency in just a matter of minutes.

This appliance has several features that make it stand out from traditional ice cream makers. For instance, the Ninja Creami has a powerful motor that enables it to freeze the mixture in a fraction of the time required by other machines. Additionally, it includes a built-in blender that can be used to create shakes and smoothies, adding to the versatility of the appliance.

A Perfect Approach To Make Cream

The Ninja Creami ice cream maker offers numerous benefits to consumers seeking a convenient and efficient method of making homemade frozen desserts.

Firstly, the Ninja Creami's powerful motor and freezing bowl combine to produce frozen desserts with a smooth and creamy consistency. This is accomplished in a fraction of the time required by traditional ice cream makers, meaning that users can enjoy their homemade desserts almost immediately.

Additionally, the Ninja Creami's user-friendly design makes it easy to use for both novice and experienced cooks. The appliance includes a variety of recipe options and flavor combinations, providing users with the opportunity to explore their creativity and experiment with different flavors and ingredients.

Another key benefit of the Ninja Creami is its versatility. It can be used to create not only ice cream, but also sorbets, gelatos, frozen yogurts, and even shakes and smoothies. This makes it an excellent investment for consumers seeking a multi-purpose appliance that can be used for a variety of different kitchen tasks.

Furthermore, the Ninja Creami is designed to be easy to clean and maintain. Its components are dishwasher safe, making cleanup a breeze, and its compact size means it can be easily stored in a standard kitchen cabinet when not in use.

No More Waiting!

In this cookbook, you will find a wide variety of recipes that are sure to delight your taste buds and impress your guests. From classic vanilla and chocolate ice cream to more adventurous flavors like green tea and lavender, there is something for everyone in this cookbook. You will also find recipes for sorbets, frozen yogurts, and even vegan and gluten-free options, so that everyone can enjoy a delicious frozen dessert.

But this cookbook is more than just a collection of recipes. It is a guide to help you master the art of making frozen desserts. You will learn about the different types of ingredients and how to use them to create the perfect texture and flavor. You will also find tips and tricks for making your desserts extra creamy, how to add mix-ins and toppings, and much more.

So, grab your Ninja Creami and let's get started on a journey of sweet and creamy indulgence!

Chapter 1 Ice Cream Mix-ins

Chapter 1 Ice Cream Mix-ins

Cookies And Coconut Ice Cream

Prep time: 5 minutes | Cook time: 3 minutes | Serves 4

1 can full-fat unsweetened coconut milk	1 teaspoon vanilla extract
½ cup organic sugar	4 chocolate sandwich cookies, crushed

1. In a medium bowl, whisk together the coconut milk, sugar, and vanilla until well combined and the sugar is dissolved. 2. Pour the base into a clean CREAMi Pint. Place the storage lid on the container and freeze for 24 hours. 3. Remove the pint from the freezer and take off the lid. Place the pint in the outer bowl of your Ninja CREAMi, install the Creamerizer Paddle in the outer bowl lid, and lock the lid assembly onto the outer bowl. Place the bowl assembly on the motor base, and twist the handle to the right to raise the platform and lock it in place. Select the Ice Cream function. 4. Once the machine has finished processing, remove the lid from the pint container. With a spoon, create a 1½-inch-wide hole that reaches the bottom of the pint. During this process, it is okay if your treat reaches above the Max Fill line. Add the crushed cookies to the hole in the pint, replace the lid, and select the Mix-In function. 5. Once the machine has finished processing, remove the ice cream from the pint. Serve immediately with desired toppings.

Birthday Cake Ice Cream

Prep time: 5 minutes | Cook time: 3 minutes | Serves 4

5 large egg yolks	1 cup heavy (whipping) cream
¼ cup corn syrup	1½ tablespoons vanilla extract
2½ tablespoons granulated sugar	3 tablespoons vanilla cake mix
⅓ cup whole milk	2 tablespoons rainbow-colored sprinkles

1. Fill a large bowl with ice water and set it aside. 2. In a small saucepan, whisk together the egg yolks, corn syrup, and sugar until the mixture is fully combined and the sugar is dissolved. Do not do this over heat. 3. Whisk in the milk, heavy cream, and vanilla. 4. Place the pan over medium heat. Cook, stirring constantly with a rubber spatula, until the temperature reaches 165°F to 175°F on an instant-read thermometer. 5. Remove the pan from the heat and pour the base through a fine-mesh strainer into a clean CREAMi Pint. Carefully place the container in the prepared ice water bath, making sure the water doesn't spill into the base. 6. Once the base has cooled, whisk in the vanilla cake mix until it is fully incorporated. Place the storage lid on the pint container and freeze for 24 hours. 7. Remove the pint from the freezer and take off the lid. Place the pint in the outer bowl of your Ninja CREAMi, install the Creamerizer Paddle in the outer bowl lid, and lock the lid assembly onto the outer bowl. Place the bowl assembly on the motor base, and twist the handle to the right to raise the platform and lock it in place. Select the Ice Cream function. 8. Once the machine has finished processing, remove the lid from the pint container. With a spoon, create a 1½-inch-wide hole that reaches the bottom of the pint. During this process, it is okay if your treat reaches above the Max Fill line. Add the rainbow sprinkles to the hole in the pint, replace the lid, and select the Mix-In function. 9. Once the machine has finished processing, remove the ice cream from the pint. Serve immediately.

Grasshopper Ice Cream

Prep time: 5 minutes | Cook time: 3 minutes | Serves 4

½ cup frozen spinach, thawed and squeezed dry	⅓ cup heavy cream
1 cup whole milk	¼ cup chocolate chunks, chopped
½ cup granulated sugar	¼ cup brownie, cut into 1-inch pieces
1 teaspoon mint extract	
3-5 drops green food coloring	

1. In a high-speed blender, add the spinach, milk, sugar, mint extract and food coloring and pulse until mixture smooth. 2. Transfer the mixture into an empty Ninja CREAMi pint container. 3. Add the heavy cream and stir until well combined. 4. Cover the container with storage lid and freeze for 24 hours. 5. After 24 hours, remove the lid from container and arrange into the Outer Bowl of Ninja CREAMi. 6. Install the Creamerizer Paddle onto the lid of Outer Bowl. 7. Then rotate the lid clockwise to lock. 8. Press Power button to turn on the unit. 9. Then press Ice Cream button. 10. When the program is completed, with a spoon, create a 1½-inch wide hole in the center that reaches the bottom of the pint container. 11. Add the chocolate chunks and brownie pieces into the hole and press Mix-In button. 12. When the program is completed, turn the Outer Bowl and release it from the machine. 13. Transfer the ice cream into serving bowls and serve immediately.

Jelly & Peanut Butter Ice Cream

Prep time: 5 minutes | Cook time: 5 minutes | Serves 4

3 tablespoons granulated sugar	¼ cup smooth peanut butter
4 large egg yolks	3 tablespoons grape jelly
1 cup whole milk	¼ cup honey roasted peanuts,
⅓ cup heavy cream	chopped

1. In a small saucepan, add the sugar and egg yolks and beat until sugar is dissolved. 2. Add the milk, heavy cream, peanut butter, and grape jelly to the saucepan and stir to combine. 3. Place saucepan over medium heat and cook until temperature reaches cook until temperature reaches to 165 -175° F, stirring continuously with a rubber spatula. 4. Remove from the heat and through a fine-mesh strainer, strain the mixture into an empty Ninja CREAMi pint container. 5. Place the container into ice bath to cool. 6. After cooling, cover the container with storage lid and freeze for 24 hours. 7. After 24 hours, remove the lid from container and arrange into the Outer Bowl of Ninja CREAMi. 8. Install the Creamerizer Paddle onto the lid of Outer Bowl. 9. Then rotate the lid clockwise to lock. 10. Press Power button to turn on the unit. 11. Then press ICE CREAM button. 12. When the program is completed, with a spoon, create a 1½-inch wide hole in the center that reaches the bottom of the pint container. 13. Add the peanuts into the hole and press Mix-In button. 14. When the program is completed, turn the Outer Bowl and release it from the machine. 15. Transfer the ice cream into serving bowls and serve immediately.

Coconut Mint Chip Ice Cream

Prep time: 5 minutes | Cook time: 3 minutes | Serves 4

1 can full-fat unsweetened coconut milk	½ teaspoon mint extract
½ cup organic sugar	¼ cup mini vegan chocolate chips

1. In a medium bowl, whisk together the coconut milk, sugar, and mint extract until everything is well combined and the sugar is dissolved. 2. Pour the base into a clean CREAMi Pint. Place the storage lid on the container and freeze for 24 hours. 3. Remove the pint from the freezer and take off the lid. Place the pint in the outer bowl of your Ninja CREAMi, install the Creamerizer Paddle in the outer bowl lid, and lock the lid assembly onto the outer bowl. Place the bowl assembly on the motor base, and twist the handle to the right to raise the platform and lock it in place. Select the Ice Cream function. 4. Once the machine has finished processing, remove the lid from the pint container. With a spoon, create a 1½-inch-wide hole that reaches the bottom of the pint. During this process, it is okay if your treat reaches above the Max Fill line. Add the mini chocolate chips to the hole in the pint, replace the lid, and select the Mix-In function. 5. Once the machine has finished processing, remove the ice cream from the pint. Serve immediately with desired toppings.

Pistachio Ice Cream

Prep time: 5 minutes | Cook time: 3 minutes | Serves 4

1 tablespoon cream cheese, softened	1 cup whole milk
⅓ cup granulated sugar	¾ cup heavy cream
1 teaspoon almond extract	¼ cup pistachios, shells removed and chopped

1. In a large microwave-safe bowl, add the cream cheese and microwave on High for about ten seconds. 2. Remove from the microwave and stir until smooth. 3. Add the sugar and almond extract and with a wire whisk, beat until the mixture looks like frosting. 4. Slowly add the milk and heavy cream and beat until well combined. 5. Transfer the mixture into an empty Ninja CREAMi pint container. 6. Cover the container with storage lid and freeze for 24 hours. 7. After 24 hours, remove the lid from container and arrange into the Outer Bowl of Ninja CREAMi. 8. Install the Creamerizer Paddle onto the lid of Outer Bowl. 9. Then rotate the lid clockwise to lock. 10. Press Power button to turn on the unit. 11. Then press Ice Cream button. 12. When the program is completed, with a spoon, create a 1½-inch wide hole in the center that reaches the bottom of the pint container. 13. Add the pistachios into the hole and press Mix-In button. 14. When the program is completed, turn the Outer Bowl and release it from the machine. 15. Transfer the ice cream into serving bowls and serve immediately.

Vanilla Ice Cream With Chocolate Chips

Prep time: 5 minutes | Cook time: 5 minutes | Serves 4

1 tablespoon cream cheese, softened	¾ cup heavy cream
⅓ cup granulated sugar	1 cup whole milk
1 teaspoon vanilla extract	¼ cup mini chocolate chips, for mix-in

1. Microwave the cream cheese for 10 seconds in a large microwave-safe bowl. With a rubber spatula, blend in the sugar and vanilla extract until the mixture resembles frosting, about 60 seconds. 2. Slowly whisk in the heavy cream and milk until smooth and the sugar has dissolved. 3. Pour the base into an empty CREAMi Pint. Place the storage lid on the Pint and freeze for 24 hours. 4. Remove the Pint from the freezer and remove the lid from the Pint. Place the Pint in the outer bowl, install the Creamerizer Paddle onto the outer bowl lid, and lock the lid assembly on the outer bowl. Select ICE CREAM. 5. With a spoon, create a 1½-inch wide hole that reaches the bottom of the Pint. During this process, it's okay for your treat to press above the max fill line. Add chocolate chips to the hole in the Pint and process again using the MIX-IN program. 6. When processing is complete, remove the ice cream from the Pint.

Bourbon-maple-walnut Ice Cream

Prep time: 5 minutes | Cook time: 3 minutes | Serves 4

4 large egg yolks	½ cup whole milk
¼ cup maple syrup	1 cup heavy (whipping) cream
¼ cup corn syrup	¼ cup toasted walnut halves
2 tablespoons bourbon	

1. Fill a large bowl with ice water and set it aside. 2. In a small saucepan, whisk together the egg yolks, maple syrup, corn syrup, and bourbon until the mixture is fully combined. Do not do this over heat. 3. Whisk in the milk and heavy cream. 4. Place the pan over medium heat. Cook, stirring constantly with a rubber spatula, until the temperature reaches 165°F to 175°F on an instant-read thermometer. 5. Remove the pan from the heat and pour the base into a clean CREAMi Pint. Carefully place the container in the prepared ice water bath, making sure the water doesn't spill into the base. 6. Once the base has cooled, place the storage lid on the pint and freeze for 24 hours. 7. Remove the pint from the freezer and take off the lid. Place the pint in the outer bowl of your Ninja CREAMi, install the Creamerizer Paddle in the outer bowl lid, and lock the lid assembly onto the outer bowl. Place the bowl assembly on the motor base, and twist the handle to the right to raise the platform and lock it in place. Select the Ice Cream function. 8. Once the machine has finished processing, remove the lid from the pint container. With a spoon, create a 1½-inch-wide hole that reaches the bottom of the pint. During this process, it is okay if your treat reaches above the Max Fill line. Add the toasted walnuts to the hole in the pint, replace the lid, and select the Mix-In function. 9. Once the machine has finished processing, remove the ice cream from the pint. Serve immediately.

Fruity Cereal Ice Cream

Prep time: 5 minutes | Cook time: 30 minutes | Serves 2

¾ cup whole milk	¼ cup granulated sugar
1 cup fruity cereal, divided	1 teaspoon vanilla extract
1 tablespoon Philadelphia cream cheese, softened	½ cup heavy cream

1. In a large mixing bowl, combine ½ cup of the fruity cereal and the milk. Allow the mixture to settle for 15–30 minutes, stirring occasionally to infuse the milk with the fruity taste. 2. Microwave the Philadelphia cream cheese for 10 seconds in a second large microwave-safe dish. Combine the sugar and vanilla extract in a mixing bowl with a whisk or rubber spatula until the mixture resembles frosting, about 60 seconds. 3. After 15 to 30 minutes, sift the milk and cereal into the bowl with the sugar mixture using a fine-mesh filter. To release extra milk, press on the cereal with a spoon, then discard it. Mix in the heavy cream until everything is thoroughly mixed. 4. Pour the mixture into an empty ninja CREAMi Pint container. Add the strawberries to the Pint, making sure not to go over the max fill line, and freeze for 24 hours. 5. After 24 hours, remove the Pint from the freezer. Remove the lid. 6. Place the Ninja CREAMi Pint into the outer bowl. Place the outer bowl with the Pint in it into the ninja CREAMi machine and turn until the outer bowl locks into place. Push the ICE CREAM button. During the ICE CREAM function, the ice cream will mix together and become very creamy. 7. Use a spoon to create a 1½-inch wide hole that reaches the bottom of the Pint. Add the remaining ½ cup of fruity cereal to the hole and process again using the mix-in. When processing is complete, remove the ice cream from the Pint.

Sneaky Mint Chip Ice Cream

Prep time: 5 minutes | Cook time: 3 minutes | Serves 4

3 large egg yolks	1 cup packed fresh spinach
1 tablespoon corn syrup	½ cup frozen peas, thawed
¼ cup granulated sugar	1 teaspoon mint extract
⅓ cup whole milk	¼ cup semisweet chocolate chips
¾ cup heavy (whipping) cream	

1. Fill a large bowl with ice water and set it aside. 2. In a small saucepan, whisk together the egg yolks, corn syrup, and sugar until the mixture is fully combined and the sugar is dissolved. Do not do this over heat. 3. Whisk in the milk and heavy cream. 4. Place the pan over medium heat. Cook, stirring constantly with a rubber spatula, until the temperature reaches 165°F to 175°F on an instant-read thermometer. 5. Remove the pan from the heat and pour the base into a clean CREAMi Pint. Carefully place the container in the prepared ice water bath, making sure the water doesn't spill into the base. 6. Once the mixture has completely cooled, pour the base into a blender and add the spinach, peas, and mint extract. Blend on high for 30 seconds. Strain the base through a fine-mesh strainer back into the CREAMi Pint. Place the storage lid on the container and freeze for 24 hours. 7. Remove the pint from the freezer and take off the lid. Place the pint in the outer bowl of your Ninja CREAMi, install the Creamerizer Paddle in the outer bowl lid, and lock the lid assembly onto the outer bowl. Place the bowl assembly on the motor base, and twist the handle to the right to raise the platform and lock it in place. Select the Ice Cream function. 8. Once the machine has finished processing, remove the lid from the pint container. With a spoon, create a 1½-inch-wide hole that reaches the bottom of the pint. During this process, it is okay if your treat reaches above the Max Fill line. Add the chocolate chips to the hole in the pint, replace the lid, and select the Mix-In function. 9. Once the machine has finished processing, remove the ice cream from the pint. Serve immediately.

Coffee Chip Ice Cream

Prep time: 5 minutes | Cook time: 3 minutes | Serves 4

¾ cup heavy cream	1 cup unsweetened almond
¼ cup monk fruit sweetener with Erythritol	milk
	1 teaspoon vanilla extract
½ teaspoon stevia sweetener	3 tablespoons chocolate chips
1½ tablespoons instant coffee granules	1 tablespoon walnuts, chopped

1. In a bowl, add the heavy cream and beat until smooth. 2. Add the remaining ingredients except for chocolate chips and walnuts and beat sweetener is dissolved. 3. Transfer the mixture into an empty Ninja CREAMi pint container. 4. Cover the container with storage lid and freeze for 24 hours. 5. After 24 hours, remove the lid from container and arrange into the Outer Bowl of Ninja CREAMi. 6. Install the Creamerizer Paddle onto the lid of Outer Bowl. 7. Then rotate the lid clockwise to lock. 8. Press Power button to turn on the unit. 9. Then press Lite Ice Cream button. 10. When the program is completed, with a spoon, create a 1½-inch wide hole in the center that reaches the bottom of the pint container. 11. Add the chocolate chips and walnuts into the hole and press Mix-In button. 12. When the program is completed, turn the Outer Bowl and release it from the machine. 13. Transfer the ice cream into serving bowls and serve immediately.

Rocky Road Ice Cream

Prep time: 5 minutes | Cook time: 3 minutes | Serves 4

1 cup whole milk	⅓ cup heavy cream
½ cup frozen cauliflower florets, thawed	2 tablespoons almonds, sliced
	2 tablespoons mini
½ cup dark brown sugar	marshmallows
3 tablespoons dark cocoa powder	2 tablespoons mini chocolate chips
1 teaspoon chocolate extract	

1. In a high-speed blender, add milk, cauliflower, brown sugar, cocoa powder, and chocolate extract and pulse until smooth. 2. Transfer the mixture into an empty Ninja CREAMi pint container. 3. Add the heavy cream and stir until well combined. 4. Cover the container with storage lid and freeze for 24 hours. 5. After 24 hours, remove the lid from container and arrange into the Outer Bowl of Ninja CREAMi. 6. Install the Creamerizer Paddle onto the lid of Outer Bowl. 7. Then rotate the lid clockwise to lock. 8. Press Power button to turn on the unit. 9. Then press Ice Cream button. 10. When the program is completed, with a spoon, create a 1½-inch wide hole in the center that reaches the bottom of the pint container. 11. Add the almonds, marshmallows and chocolate chips into the hole and press Mix-In button. 12. When the program is completed, turn the Outer Bowl and release it from the machine. 13. Transfer the ice cream into serving bowls and serve immediately.

Cookies & Cream Ice Cream

Prep time: 5 minutes | Cook time: 5 minutes | Serves 2

½ tablespoon cream cheese, softened	½ cup heavy cream
	½ cup whole milk
¼ cup granulated sugar	1½ chocolate sandwich cookies,
½ teaspoon vanilla extract	broken, for mix-in

1. Microwave the cream cheese for 10 seconds in a large microwave-safe bowl. Combine the sugar and vanilla extract in a mixing bowl and whisk or scrape together until the mixture resembles frosting, about 60 seconds. 2. Slowly whisk in the heavy cream and milk until smooth and the sugar has dissolved. 3. Pour the base into an empty CREAMi Pint. Place storage lid on the Pint and freeze for 24 hours. 4. Remove the Pint from the freezer and remove the lid from the Pint. Place the Pint in the outer bowl, install Creamerizer Paddle onto the outer bowl lid, and lock the lid assembly on the outer bowl. Select ICE CREAM. 5. With a spoon, create a 1½-inch wide hole that reaches the bottom of the Pint. During this process, it's okay for your treat to go above the max fill line. Add the broken chocolate sandwich cookies to the hole and process again using the MIX-IN program. 6. When processing is complete, remove the ice cream from the Pint and serve immediately.

Mint Cookies Ice Cream

Prep time: 5 minutes | Cook time: 3 minutes | Serves 4

¾ cup coconut cream	5-6 drops green food coloring
¼ cup monk fruit sweetener with Erythritol	1 cup oat milk
	3 chocolate sandwich cookies,
2 tablespoons agave nectar	quartered
½ teaspoon mint extract	

1. In a large bowl, add the coconut cream and beat until smooth. 2. Add the sweetener, agave nectar, mint extract and food coloring and beat until sweetener is dissolved. 3. Add the oat milk and beat until well combined. 4. Transfer the mixture into an empty Ninja CREAMi pint container. 5. Cover the container with storage lid and freeze for 24 hours. 6. After 24 hours, remove the lid from container and arrange into the Outer Bowl of Ninja CREAMi. 7. Install the Creamerizer Paddle onto the lid of Outer Bowl. 8. Then rotate the lid clockwise to lock. 9. Press Power button to turn on the unit. 10. Then press Lite Ice Cream button. 11. When the program is completed, with a spoon, create a 1½-inch wide hole in the center that reaches the bottom of the pint container. 12. Add the cookie pieces into the hole and press Mix-In button. 13. When the program is completed, turn the Outer Bowl and release it from the machine. 14. Transfer the ice cream into serving bowls and serve immediately.

Chocolate Brownie Ice Cream

Prep time: 5 minutes | Cook time: 3 minutes | Serves 4

1 tablespoon cream cheese, softened	1 cup whole milk
⅓ cup granulated sugar	¾ cup heavy cream
1 teaspoon vanilla extract	2 tablespoons mini chocolate chips
2 tablespoons cocoa powder	2 tablespoons brownie chunks

1. In a large microwave-safe bowl, add the cream cheese and microwave on High for about ten seconds. 2. Remove from the microwave and stir until smooth. 3. Add the sugar and almond extract and with a wire whisk, beat until the mixture looks like frosting. 4. Slowly add the milk and heavy cream and beat until well combined. 5. Transfer the mixture into an empty Ninja CREAMi pint container. 6. Cover the container with storage lid and freeze for 24 hours. 7. After 24 hours, remove the lid from container and arrange into the Outer Bowl of Ninja CREAMi. 8. Install the Creamerizer Paddle onto the lid of Outer Bowl. 9. Then rotate the lid clockwise to lock. 10. Press Power button to turn on the unit. 11. Then press Ice Cream button. 12. When the program is completed, with a spoon, create a 1½-inch wide hole in the center that reaches the bottom of the pint container. 13. Add the chocolate chunks and brownie pieces into the hole and press Mix-In button. 14. When the program is completed, turn the Outer Bowl and release it from the machine. 15. Transfer the ice cream into serving bowls and serve immediately.

Triple-chocolate Ice Cream

Prep time: 5 minutes | Cook time: 3 minutes | Serves 4

4 large egg yolks	¾ cup heavy (whipping) cream
⅓ cup granulated sugar	½ cup whole milk
1 tablespoon unsweetened cocoa powder	1 teaspoon vanilla extract
1 tablespoon hot fudge sauce	¼ cup white chocolate chips

1. Fill a large bowl with ice water and set it aside. 2. In a small saucepan, whisk together the egg yolks, sugar, and cocoa powder until the mixture is fully combined and the sugar is dissolved. Do not do this over heat. 3. Whisk in the hot fudge, heavy cream, milk, and vanilla. 4. Place the pan over medium heat. Cook, stirring constantly with a rubber spatula, until the temperature reaches 165°F to 175°F on an instant-read thermometer. 5. Remove the pan from the heat and pour the base through a fine-mesh strainer into a clean CREAMi Pint. Carefully place the container in the prepared ice water bath, making sure the water doesn't spill into the base. 6. Once the base has cooled, place the storage lid on the pint and freeze for 24 hours. 7. Remove the pint from the freezer and take off the lid. Place the pint in the outer bowl of your Ninja CREAMi, install the Creamerizer Paddle in the outer bowl lid, and lock the lid assembly onto the outer bowl. Place the bowl assembly on the motor base, and twist the handle to the right to raise the platform and lock it in place. Select the Ice Cream function. 8. Once the machine has finished processing, remove the lid from the pint container. With a spoon, create a 1½-inch-wide hole that reaches the bottom of the pint. During this process, it is okay if your treat reaches above the Max Fill line. Add the white chocolate chips to the hole in the pint, replace the lid, and select the Mix-In function. 9. Once the machine has finished processing, remove the ice cream from the pint. Serve immediately with desired toppings.

Lite Chocolate Cookie Ice Cream

Prep time: 5 minutes | Cook time: 5 minutes | Serves 2

1 tablespoon cream cheese, at room temperature	1 teaspoon vanilla extract
2 tablespoons unsweetened cocoa powder	¾ cup heavy cream
	1 cup whole milk
½ teaspoon stevia sweetener	¼ cup crushed reduced-fat sugar cookies
3 tablespoons raw agave nectar	

1. Place the cream cheese in a large microwave-safe bowl and heat on high for 10 seconds. 2. Mix in the cocoa powder, stevia, agave, and vanilla. Microwave for 60 seconds more, or until the mixture resembles frosting. 3. Slowly whisk in the heavy cream and milk until the sugar has dissolved and the mixture is thoroughly mixed. 4. Pour the base into a clean CREAMi Pint. Place the storage lid on the container and freeze for 24 hours. 5. Remove the Pint from the freezer and take off the lid. Place the Pint in the outer bowl of your Ninja CREAMi, install the Creamerizer Paddle in the outer bowl lid, and lock the lid assembly onto the outer bowl. Place the bowl assembly on the motor base, and twist the handle to the right to raise the platform and lock it in place. Select the LITE ICE CREAM function. 6. Once the machine has finished processing, remove the lid. With a spoon, create a 1½-inch-wide hole that reaches the bottom of the Pint. During this process, it's okay if your treat goes above the max fill line. Add the crushed cookies to the hole in the Pint. Replace the Pint lid and select the MIX-IN function. 7. Once the machine has finished processing, remove the ice cream from the Pint.

Rum Raisin Ice Cream

Prep time: 5 minutes | Cook time: 23 minutes | Serves 4

3 large egg yolks	1 cup whole milk
¼ cup dark brown sugar (or coconut sugar)	1 teaspoon rum extract
1 tablespoon light corn syrup	⅓ cup raisins
½ cup heavy cream	¼ cup dark or spiced rum

1. In a small saucepan, combine the egg yolks, sugar, and corn syrup. Whisk until everything is well mixed and the sugar has dissolved. Whisk together the heavy cream and milk until smooth. 2. Stir the mixture frequently with a whisk or a rubber spatula in a saucepan over medium-low heat. Using an instant-read thermometer, cook until the temperature hits 165°F–175°F. 3. Remove the base from heat, stir in the rum extract, then pour through a fine-mesh strainer into an empty CREAMi Pint. Place into an ice bath. Once cooled, place the storage lid on the Pint and freeze for 24 hours. 4. While the base is cooling, prepare the mix-in. Add the raisins and rum to a small bowl and microwave for 1 minute. Let cool, then drain the remaining rum. Cover and set aside. 5. Remove the Pint from the freezer and remove its lid. Place the Pint in the outer bowl, install the Creamerizer Paddle onto the outer bowl lid, and lock the lid assembly on the outer bowl. Select ICE CREAM. 6. With a spoon, create a 1½-inch wide hole that reaches the bottom of the Pint. Add the mixed raisins to the hole and process again using the MIX-IN program. 7. When processing is complete, remove the ice cream from the Pint.

Lavender Cookie Ice Cream

Prep time: 5 minutes | Cook time: 10 minutes | Serves 4

¾ cup heavy cream	½ cup sweetened condensed milk
1 tablespoon dried culinary lavender	4 drops purple food coloring
⅛ teaspoon salt	⅓ cup chocolate wafer cookies, crushed
¾ cup whole milk	

1. In a medium saucepan, add heavy cream, lavender and salt and mix well. 2. Place the saucepan over low heat and steep, covered for about ten minutes, stirring after every two minutes. 3. Remove from the heat and through a fine-mesh strainer, strain the cream mixture into a large bowl. 4. Discard the lavender leaves. 5. In the bowl of cream mixture, add the milk, condensed milk and purple food coloring and beat until smooth. 6. Transfer the mixture into an empty Ninja CREAMi pint container. 7. Cover the container with storage lid and freeze for 24 hours. 8. After 24 hours, remove the lid from container and arrange into the Outer Bowl of Ninja CREAMi. 9. Install the Creamerizer Paddle onto the lid of Outer Bowl. 10. Then rotate the lid clockwise to lock. 11. Press Power button to turn on the unit. 12. Then press Ice Cream button. 13. When the program is completed, with a spoon, create a 1½-inch wide hole in the center that reaches the bottom of the pint container. 14. Add the crushed cookies the hole and press Mix-In button. 15. When the program is completed, turn the Outer Bowl and release it from the machine. 16. Transfer the ice cream into serving bowls and serve immediately.

Sweet Potato Pie Ice Cream

Prep time: 5 minutes | Cook time: 3 minutes | Serves 4

1 cup canned pureed sweet potato	1 teaspoon vanilla extract
1 tablespoon corn syrup	1 teaspoon cinnamon
¼ cup plus 1 tablespoon light brown sugar	¾ cup heavy (whipping) cream
	¼ cup mini marshmallows

1. Combine the sweet potato puree, corn syrup, brown sugar, vanilla, and cinnamon in a blender. Blend on high until smooth. 2. Pour the base into a clean CREAMi Pint. Whisk in the heavy cream until combined. Place the storage lid on the container and freeze for 24 hours. 3. Remove the pint from the freezer and take off the lid. Place the pint in the outer bowl of your Ninja CREAMi, install the Creamerizer Paddle in the outer bowl lid, and lock the lid assembly onto the outer bowl. Place the bowl assembly on the motor base, and twist the handle to the right to raise the platform and lock it in place. Select the Ice Cream function. 4. Once the machine has finished processing, remove the lid from the pint container. With a spoon, create a 1½-inch-wide hole that reaches the bottom of the pint. During this process, it is okay if your treat reaches above the Max Fill line. Add the marshmallows to the hole in the pint, replace the lid, and select the Mix-In function. 5. Once the machine has finished processing, remove the ice cream from the pint. Serve immediately with desired toppings.

Chapter 2 Ice Cream Recipes

Chapter 2 Ice Cream Recipes

Kale'd By Chocolate Ice Cream

Prep time: 5 minutes | Cook time: 5 minutes | Serves 4

1 cup frozen kale	3 tablespoons dark unsweetened
1 tablespoon cream cheese, at	cocoa powder
room temperature	¾ cup whole milk
⅓ cup granulated sugar	¾ cup heavy (whipping) cream

1. Combine the frozen kale, cream cheese, sugar, cocoa powder, and milk in a blender. Blend on high until smooth. 2. Pour the base into a clean CREAMi Pint. Whisk in the heavy cream until combined. Place the storage lid on the container and freeze for 24 hours. 3. Remove the CREAMi Pint from the freezer and take off the lid. Place the pint in the outer bowl of your Ninja CREAMi, install the Creamerizer Paddle in outer bowl lid, and lock the lid assembly onto the outer bowl. Place the bowl assembly on the motor base, and twist the handle to the right to raise the platform and lock it in place. Select the Ice Cream function. 4. Once the machine has finished processing, remove the ice cream from the pint. Serve immediately with desired toppings.

Strawberry-carrot Ice Cream

Prep time: 5 minutes | Cook time: 5 minutes | Serves 4

1 cup frozen carrot slices,	⅓ cup granulated sugar
thawed	1 teaspoon strawberry extract
½ cup trimmed and quartered	½ cup whole milk
fresh strawberries	5 drops red food coloring
1 tablespoon cream cheese, at	½ cup heavy (whipping) cream
room temperature	

1. Combine the carrots, strawberries, cream cheese, sugar, strawberry extract, milk, and food coloring in a blender. Blend on high until smooth. 2. Pour the base into a clean CREAMi Pint. Whisk in the heavy cream until combined. Place the storage lid on the container and freeze for 24 hours. 3. Remove the CREAMi Pint from the freezer and take off the lid. Place the pint in the outer bowl of your Ninja CREAMi, install the Creamerizer Paddle in the outer bowl lid, and lock the lid assembly onto the outer bowl. Place the bowl assembly on the motor base, and twist the handle to the right to raise the platform and lock it in place. Select the Ice Cream function. 4. Once the machine has finished processing, remove the ice cream from the pint. Serve immediately with desired toppings.

Super Lemon Ice Cream

Prep time: 5 minutes | Cook time: 20 minutes | Serves 5

1 cup heavy whipping cream	1 tablespoon grated lemon zest
½ cup half-and-half cream	2 egg yolks
½ cup white sugar	¼ cup fresh lemon juice

1. On low heat, whisk together the heavy cream, half-and-half cream, sugar, and lemon zest in a saucepan until the sugar is dissolved. 2. In a mixing dish, whisk together the egg yolks. 3. Stir in a few tablespoons of the cream mixture at a time into the eggs. This will assist in bringing the eggs up to temperature without them becoming scrambled. Return the egg mixture to the bowl with the cream mixture. 4. Pour the mixture into an empty ninja CREAMi Pint container, add lemon, and freeze for 24 hours. 5. After 24 hours, remove the Pint from the freezer. Remove the lid. 6. Place the Ninja CREAMi Pint into the outer bowl. Place the outer bowl with the Pint in it into the ninja CREAMi machine and turn until the outer bowl locks into place. Push the ICE CREAM button. 7. Once the ICE CREAM function has ended, turn the outer bowl and release it from the ninja CREAMi machine.

Coffee Ice Cream

Prep time: 5 minutes | Cook time: 5 minutes | Serves 4

¾ cup coconut cream	powder
½ cup granulated sugar	1 cup rice milk
1½ tablespoons instant coffee	1 teaspoon vanilla extract

1. In a bowl, add coconut cream and beat until smooth. 2. Add the remaining ingredients and beat sugar is dissolved. 3. Transfer the mixture into an empty Ninja CREAMi pint container. 4. Cover the container with storage lid and freeze for 24 hours. 5. After 24 hours, remove the lid from container and arrange into the Outer Bowl of Ninja CREAMi. 6. Install the Creamerizer Paddle onto the lid of Outer Bowl. 7. Then rotate the lid clockwise to lock. 8. Press Power button to turn on the unit. 9. Then press Ice Cream button. 10. When the program is completed, turn the Outer Bowl and release it from the machine. 11. Transfer the ice cream into serving bowls and serve immediately.

Strawberry Ice Cream

Prep time: 5 minutes | Cook time: 5 minutes | Serves 4

¼ cup sugar

1 tablespoon cream cheese, softened

1 teaspoon vanilla bean paste

1 cup milk

¾ cup heavy whipping cream

6 medium fresh strawberries, hulled and quartered

1. In a bowl, add the sugar, cream cheese, vanilla bean paste and with a wire whisk, mix until well combined. 2. Add in the milk and heavy whipping cream and beat until well combined. 3. Transfer the mixture into an empty Ninja CREAMi pint container. 4. Add the strawberry pieces and stir to combine. 5. Cover the container with storage lid and freeze for 24 hours. 6. After 24 hours, remove the lid from container and arrange into the Outer Bowl of Ninja CREAMi. 7. Install the Creamerizer Paddle onto the lid of Outer Bowl. 8. Then rotate the lid clockwise to lock. 9. Press Power button to turn on the unit. 10. Then press Ice Cream button. 11. When the program is completed, turn the Outer Bowl and release it from the machine. 12. Transfer the ice cream into serving bowls and serve immediately.

Classic Vanilla Ice Cream

Prep time: 5 minutes | Cook time: 5 minutes | Serves 4

1 tablespoon cream cheese, at room temperature

⅓ cup granulated sugar

1 teaspoon vanilla extract

¾ cup heavy (whipping) cream

1 cup whole milk

¼ cup mini chocolate chips (optional)

1. In a large microwave-safe bowl, add the cream cheese and microwave for 10 seconds. Add the sugar and vanilla extract, and with a whisk or rubber spatula, combine the mixture until it looks like frosting, about 60 seconds. 2. Slowly whisk in the heavy cream and milk and mix until the sugar is completely dissolved and the cream cheese is completely incorporated. 3. Pour the base into a clean CREAMi Pint. Place the storage lid on the container and freeze for 24 hours. 4. Remove the CREAMi Pint from the freezer and take off the lid. Place the pint container in the outer bowl of your Ninja CREAMi, install the Creamerizer Paddle in the outer bowl lid, and lock the lid assembly onto the outer bowl. Place the bowl assembly on the motor base, and twist the handle to the right to raise the platform and lock it in place. Select the Ice Cream function. 5. Once the machine has finished processing, remove the lid from the pint container. If you are adding chocolate chips: with a spoon, create a 1½-inch-wide hole that reaches the bottom of the pint. During this process, it is okay if your treat reaches above the Max Fill line. Add ¼ cup of mini chocolate chips to the hole in the pint, replace the lid, and select the Mix-In function. 6. Serve immediately with desired toppings.

Sea Salt Caramel Ice Cream

Prep time: 5 minutes | Cook time: 5 minutes | Serves 4

4 large egg yolks

1 tablespoon dark brown sugar

3 tablespoons prepared caramel sauce

⅓ cup whole milk

1 cup heavy (whipping) cream

1 teaspoon sea salt

1. Fill a large bowl with ice water and set it aside. 2. In a small saucepan, whisk the egg yolks, brown sugar, and caramel sauce until the mixture is fully combined and the sugar is dissolved. Do not do this over heat. 3. Whisk in the milk, heavy cream, and sea salt until combined. 4. Place the pan over medium heat. Using a rubber spatula, stir constantly and cook until the temperature reaches 165°F to 175°F on an instant-read thermometer. 5. Remove the pan from the heat and pour the base through a fine-mesh strainer into a CREAMi Pint. Carefully place the pint in the prepared ice water bath, making sure the water doesn't spill into the base. 6. Once the base has cooled, place the storage lid on the pint container and freeze for 24 hours. 7. Remove the CREAMi Pint from the freezer and take off the lid. Place the pint in the outer bowl of your Ninja CREAMi, install the Creamerizer Paddle in the outer bowl lid, and lock the lid assembly onto the outer bowl. Place the bowl assembly on the motor base, and twist the handle to the right to raise the platform and lock it in place. Select the Ice Cream function. 8. Once the machine has finished processing, remove the ice cream from the pint. Serve immediately with desired toppings.

Earl Grey Tea Ice Cream

Prep time: 5 minutes | Cook time: 25 minutes | Serves 4

1 cup heavy cream

1 cup whole milk

5 tablespoons monk fruit

sweetener

3 Earl Grey tea bags

1. In a medium saucepan, add cream and milk and stir to combine. 2. Place saucepan over medium heat and cook until for bout two-three minutes or until steam is rising. 3. Stir in the monk fruit sweetener and reduce the heat to very low. 4. Add teabags and cover the saucepan for about 20 minutes. 5. Discard the tea bags and remove saucepan from heat. 6. Transfer the mixture into an empty Ninja CREAMi pint container and place into an ice bath to cool. 7. After cooling, cover the container with storage lid and freeze for 24 hours. 8. After 24 hours, remove the lid from container and arrange into the Outer Bowl of Ninja CREAMi. 9. Install the Creamerizer Paddle onto the lid of Outer Bowl. 10. Then rotate the lid clockwise to lock. 11. Press Power button to turn on the unit. 12. Then press Ice Cream button. 13. When the program is completed, turn the Outer Bowl and release it from the machine. 14. Transfer the ice cream into serving bowls and serve immediately.

Creamy Caramel Macchiato Coffee Ice Cream

Prep time: 5 minutes | Cook time: 5 minutes | Serves 6

1 cup heavy whipping cream	(liquid creamer)
½ cup sweetened condensed milk	1 teaspoon instant coffee granules
¼ cup coffee-mate caramel macchiato flavored creamer	Caramel syrup (for drizzling)

1. Combine all ingredients (except the syrup) in a big mixing bowl of a stand mixer or a large mixing dish. 2. Whip the heavy cream mixture with an electric mixer until firm peaks form (to prevent massive splattering, start at a slower speed, and as the cream thickens, increase the speed). Make sure the whip cream mixture isn't overmixed or "broken." 3. Pour the mixture into an empty ninja CREAMi Pint container and freeze for 24 hours. 4. After 24 hours, remove the Pint from the freezer. Remove the lid. 5. Place the Ninja CREAMi Pint into the outer bowl. Place the outer bowl with the Pint in it into the ninja CREAMi machine and turn until the outer bowl locks into place. Push the ICE CREAM button. 6. Once the ICE CREAM function has ended, turn the outer bowl and release it from the ninja CREAMi machine.

Peanut Butter & Jelly Ice Cream

Prep time: 5 minutes | Cook time: 5 minutes | Serves 4

3 tablespoons granulated sugar	¼ cup smooth peanut butter
4 large egg yolks	3 tablespoons grape jelly
1 cup whole milk	¼ cup honey roasted peanuts, chopped
⅓ cup heavy cream	

1. In a small saucepan, add the sugar and egg yolks and beat until well combined. 2. Add the milk, heavy cream, peanut butter, and grape jelly to the saucepan and stir to combine. 3. Place saucepan over medium heat and for about 3-5 minutes, stirring continuously. 4. Remove from the heat and through a fine-mesh strainer, strain the mixture into an empty Ninja CREAMi pint container. 5. Place the container into an ice bath to cool. 6. After cooling, cover the container with the storage lid and freeze for 24 hours. 7. After 24 hours, remove the lid from container and arrange into the outer bowl of Ninja CREAMi. 8. Install the "Creamerizer Paddle" onto the lid of outer bowl. 9. Then rotate the lid clockwise to lock. 10. Press "Power" button to turn on the unit. 11. Then press "ICE CREAM" button. 12. When the program is completed, with a spoon, create a 1½-inch wide hole in the center that reaches the bottom of the pint container. 13. Add the peanuts into the hole and press "MIX-IN" button. 14. When the program is completed, turn the outer bowl and release it from the machine. 15. Transfer the ice cream into serving bowls and serve immediately.

Mango Ice Cream

Prep time: 5 minutes | Cook time: 5 minutes | Serves 1

1 mango (medium-sized, cut into quarters)	¼ cup sugar
1 tablespoon cream cheese (room temperature)	¾ cup heavy whipping cream
	1 cup milk

1. Combine the cream cheese, sugar in a mixing bowl. Using a whisk, mix together until all ingredients are thoroughly combined, and the sugar starts to dissolve. 2. Add in the heavy whipping cream and milk. Whisk until all ingredients have combined well. 3. Pour mixture into an empty ninja CREAMi Pint container. Freeze for 24 hours after adding the mango to the Pint, ensuring you don't go over the maximum fill line. 4. Take the Pint out of the freezer after 24 hours. Take off the cover. 5. Place the Ninja CREAMi Pint into the outer bowl. Place the outer bowl with the Pint in it into the ninja CREAMi machine and turn until the outer bowl locks into place. Push the ICE CREAM button. During the ICE CREAM function, the ice cream will mix and become very creamy. 11. Once the ICE CREAM function has ended, turn the outer bowl and release it from the ninja CREAMi machine.

Mint Cookie Ice Cream

Prep time: 5 minutes | Cook time: 5 minutes | Serves 4

¾ cup coconut cream	5-6 drops green food coloring
¼ cup monk fruit sweetener with Erythritol	1 cup oat milk
2 tablespoons agave nectar	3 chocolate sandwich cookies, quartered
½ teaspoon mint extract	

1. In a large bowl, add the coconut cream and beat until smooth. 2. Add the sweetener, agave nectar, mint extract and food coloring and beat until sweetener is dissolved. 3. Add the oat milk and beat until well combined. 4. Transfer the mixture into an empty Ninja CREAMi pint container. 5. Cover the container with the storage lid and freeze for 24 hours. 6. After 24 hours, remove the lid from container and arrange into the outer bowl of Ninja CREAMi. 7. Install the "Creamerizer Paddle" onto the lid of outer bowl. 8. Then rotate the lid clockwise to lock. 9. Press "Power" button to turn on the unit. 10. Then press "LITE ICE CREAM" button. 11. When the program is completed, with a spoon, create a 1½-inch wide hole in the center that reaches the bottom of the pint container. 12. Add the cookie pieces into the hole and press "MIX-IN" button. 13. When the program is completed, turn the outer bowl and release it from the machine. 14. Transfer the ice cream into serving bowls and serve immediately.

Blueberry Ice Cream

Prep time: 5 minutes | Cook time: 5 minutes | Serves 4

1 cup blueberries	¼ cup milk
½ cup vanilla whole milk Greek yogurt	2 tablespoons honey
	2 tablespoons chia seeds

1. In a bowl, add all ingredients and eat until well combined. 2. Transfer the mixture into an empty Ninja CREAMi pint container. 3. Cover the container with storage lid and freeze for 24 hours. 4. After 24 hours, remove the lid from container and arrange into the Outer Bowl of Ninja CREAMi. 5. Install the Creamerizer Paddle onto the lid of Outer Bowl. 6. Then rotate the lid clockwise to lock. 7. Press Power button to turn on the unit. 8. Then press Ice Cream button. 9. When the program is completed, turn the Outer Bowl and release it from the machine. 10. Transfer the ice cream into serving bowls and serve immediately.

Peanut Butter Ice Cream

Prep time: 5 minutes | Cook time: 5 minutes | Serves 4

1¾ cups skim milk	¼ cup stevia-cane sugar blend
3 tablespoons smooth peanut butter	1 teaspoon vanilla extract

1. In a bowl, add all ingredients and beat until smooth. 2. Set aside for about five minutes. 3. Transfer the mixture into an empty Ninja CREAMi pint container. 4. Cover the container with storage lid and freeze for 24 hours. 5. After 24 hours, remove the lid from container and arrange into the outer bowl of Ninja CREAMi. 6. Install the Creamerizer Paddle onto the lid of Outer Bowl. 7. Then rotate the lid clockwise to lock. 8. Press Power button to turn on the unit. 9. Then press Ice Cream button. 10. When the program is completed, turn the Outer Bowl and release it from the machine. 11. Transfer the ice cream into serving bowls and serve immediately.

Matcha Ice Cream

Prep time: 5 minutes | Cook time: 10 seconds | Serves 4

1 tablespoon cream cheese, softened	1 teaspoon vanilla extract
⅓ cup granulated sugar	1 cup whole milk
2 tablespoons matcha powder	¾ cup heavy cream

1. In a large microwave-safe bowl, add the cream cheese and microwave for on High for about ten seconds. 2. Remove from the microwave and stir until smooth. 3. Add the sugar, matcha powder and vanilla extract and with a wire whisk, beat until the mixture looks like frosting. 4. Slowly add the milk and heavy cream and beat until well combined. 5. Transfer the mixture into an empty Ninja CREAMi pint container. 6. Cover the container with storage lid and freeze for 24 hours. 7. After 24 hours, remove the lid from container and arrange into the Outer Bowl of Ninja CREAMi. 8. Install the Creamerizer Paddle onto the lid of Outer Bowl. 9. Then rotate the lid clockwise to lock. 10. Press Power button to turn on the unit. 11. Then press Ice Cream button. 12. When the program is completed, turn the Outer Bowl and release it from the machine. 13. Transfer the ice cream into serving bowls and serve immediately.

Cherry-chocolate Chunk Ice Cream

Prep time: 5 minutes | Cook time: 10 minutes | Serves 4

1 packet frozen sweet cherries	1 teaspoon vanilla extract
¾ cup heavy cream	1 bar semisweet baking chocolate, broken into small chunks
1 can sweetened condensed milk	
½ cup milk	

1. Combine the heavy cream, sweetened condensed milk, milk, and vanilla extract in a mixing bowl. 2. Pour the ice cream mixture into an empty ninja CREAMi Pint container, add the chopped cherries and chocolate chunks, and freeze for 24 hours. 3. After 24 hours, remove the Pint from the freezer. Remove the lid. 4. Place the Ninja CREAMi Pint into the outer bowl. Place the outer bowl with the Pint in it into the ninja CREAMi machine and turn until the outer bowl locks into place. Push the ICE CREAM button. 5. Once the ICE CREAM function has ended, turn the outer bowl and release it from the ninja CREAMi machine.

Pumpkin Gingersnap Ice Cream

Prep time: 5 minutes | Cook time: 15 minutes | Serves 4

1 cup heavy whipping cream	1 can Eagle Brand sweetened condensed milk
½ tablespoon vanilla extract	
½ teaspoon ground cinnamon	½ cup crushed gingersnap cookies
½ teaspoon ground ginger	
½ cup solid-pack pumpkin	

1. In a large mixing bowl, beat the heavy whipping cream, vanilla extract, cinnamon, and ginger with an electric mixer on medium speed until stiff peaks form. 2. Combine the pumpkin and sweetened condensed milk in a mixing bowl. 3. Add the crushed gingersnap cookies to the pumpkin mixture and stir well. 4. Pour the mixture into an empty ninja CREAMi Pint container and freeze for 24 hours. 5. After 24 hours, remove the Pint from the freezer. Remove the lid. 6. Place the Ninja CREAMi Pint into the outer bowl. Place the outer bowl with the Pint in it into the ninja CREAMi machine and turn until the outer bowl locks into place. Push the ICE CREAM button. 7. Once the ICE CREAM function has ended, turn the outer bowl and release it from the ninja CREAMi machine.

Coconut Ice Cream

Prep time: 5 minutes | Cook time: 5 minutes | Serves 4

½ cup milk

1 can cream of coconut

¾ cup heavy cream

½ cup sweetened flaked coconut

1. In a food processor or blender, combine the milk and coconut cream and thoroughly mix. 2. Combine the heavy cream and flaked coconut in a mixing bowl, and then add to the milk-cream mixture. Combine well. 3. Pour the mixture into an empty ninja CREAMi Pint container and freeze for 24 hours. 4. After 24 hours, remove the Pint from the freezer. Remove the lid. 5. Place the Ninja CREAMi Pint into the outer bowl. Place the outer bowl with the Pint in it into the ninja CREAMi machine and turn until the outer bowl locks into place. Push the ICE CREAM button. 6. Once the ICE CREAM function has ended, turn the outer bowl and release it from the ninja CREAMi machine.

Low-sugar Vanilla Ice Cream

Prep time: 5 minutes | Cook time: 5 minutes | Serves 4

1¾ cup fat-free half-and-half

¼ cup stevia cane sugar blend

1 teaspoon vanilla extract

1. In a medium bowl, whisk the half-and-half, sugar, and vanilla together until everything is combined and the sugar is dissolved. The mixture will be foamy. Let it sit for 5 minutes or until the foam subsides. 2. Pour the base into a clean CREAMi Pint. Place the storage lid on the container and freeze for 24 hours. 3. Remove the CREAMi Pint from the freezer and take off the lid. Place the pint in the outer bowl of your Ninja CREAMi, install the Creamerizer Paddle in the outer bowl lid, and lock the lid assembly onto the outer bowl. Place the bowl assembly on the motor base, and twist the handle to the right to raise the platform and lock it in place. Select the Lite Ice Cream function. 4. Once the machine has finished processing, remove the ice cream from the pint. Serve immediately.

Cinnamon Red Hot Ice Cream

Prep time: 5 minutes | Cook time: 10 minutes | Serves 5

2 cups heavy whipping cream, divided

1 egg yolk

1 cup half-and-half

½ cup Red Hot candies

1. In a mixing bowl, whisk together 1 cup of cream and the egg yolks until smooth. 2. In another large bowl, combine the half-and-half, 1 cup cream, and Red Hot candies. Whisk with a wooden spoon until the candies dissolve, about 5 to 10 minutes. 3. Pour the cream-egg mixture into the candy mixture and stir to incorporate. 4. Pour the mixture into an empty ninja CREAMi Pint container and freeze for 24 hours. 5. After 24 hours, remove the Pint from the freezer. Remove the lid. 6. Place the Ninja CREAMi Pint into the outer bowl. Place the outer bowl with the Pint in it into the ninja CREAMi machine and turn until the outer bowl locks into place. Push the ICE CREAM button. 7. Once the ICE CREAM function has ended, turn the outer bowl and release it from the ninja CREAMi machine.

Lemon Ice Cream

Prep time: 5 minutes | Cook time: 5 minutes | Serves 4

1 can full-fat unsweetened coconut milk

½ cup granulated sugar

1 teaspoon vanilla extract

1 teaspoon lemon extract

1. In a bowl, add the coconut milk and beat until smooth. 2. Add the remaining ingredients and beat until sugar is dissolved. 3. Transfer the mixture into an empty Ninja CREAMi pint container. 4. Cover the container with storage lid and freeze for 24 hours. 5. After 24 hours, remove the lid from container and arrange into the Outer Bowl of Ninja CREAMi. 6. Install the Creamerizer Paddle onto the lid of Outer Bowl. 7. Then rotate the lid clockwise to lock. 8. Press Power button to turn on the unit. 9. Then press Ice Cream button. 10. When the program is completed, turn the Outer Bowl and release it from the machine. 11. Transfer the ice cream into serving bowls and serve immediately.

Philadelphia-style Chocolate Ice Cream

Prep time: 5 minutes | Cook time: 5 minutes | Serves 4

1 tablespoon cream cheese, at room temperature

1 tablespoon unsweetened cocoa powder

⅓ cup granulated sugar

1 teaspoon vanilla extract

¾ cup heavy (whipping) cream

1 cup whole milk

1. In a large microwave-safe bowl, add the cream cheese and microwave for 10 seconds. Add the cocoa powder, sugar, and vanilla extract, and with a whisk or rubber spatula, combine the mixture until it looks like frosting, about 60 seconds. 2. Slowly mix in the heavy cream and milk until everything is fully combined and the sugar is dissolved. 3. Pour the base into a clean CREAMi Pint. Place the storage lid on the container and freeze for 24 hours. 4. Remove the CREAMi Pint from the freezer and take off the lid. Place the pint in the outer bowl of your Ninja CREAMi, install the Creamerizer Paddle in the outer bowl lid, and lock the lid assembly onto the outer bowl. Place the bowl assembly on the motor base, and twist the handle to the right to raise the platform and lock it in place. Select the Ice Cream function. 5. Once the machine has finished processing, remove the ice cream from the pint. Serve immediately with desired toppings.

Carrot Ice Cream

Prep time: 5 minutes | Cook time: 1 minutes | Serves 2

1 cup heavy cream	frosting
½ cup carrot juice	1 teaspoon vanilla extract
⅓ cup light brown sugar	1 teaspoon ground cinnamon
2 tablespoons cream cheese	

1. In a bowl, add all ingredients and beat until well combined. 2. Transfer the mixture into an empty Ninja CREAMi pint container. 3. Cover the container with the storage lid and freeze for 24 hours 4. After 24 hours, remove the lid from container and arrange into the outer bowl of Ninja CREAMi. 5. Install the "Creamerizer Paddle" onto the lid of outer bowl. 6. Then rotate the lid clockwise to lock. 7. Press "Power" button to turn on the unit. 8. Then press "ICE CREAM" button. 9. When the program is completed, turn the outer bowl and release it from the machine. 10. Transfer the ice cream into serving bowls and serve immediately.

Fruity Extract Ice Cream

Prep time: 5 minutes | Cook time: 5 minutes | Serves 4

1 cup whole milk	½ teaspoon raspberry extract
¾ cup heavy cream	½ teaspoon vanilla extract
2 tablespoons monk fruit sweetener with Erythritol	¼ teaspoon lemon extract
2 tablespoons agave nectar	5-6 drops blue food coloring

1. In a bowl, add all ingredients and eat until well combined. 2. Transfer the mixture into an empty Ninja CREAMi pint container. 3. Cover the container with storage lid and freeze for 24 hours. 4. After 24 hours, remove the lid from container and arrange into the Outer Bowl of Ninja CREAMi. 5. Install the Creamerizer Paddle onto the lid of outer bowl. 6. Then rotate the lid clockwise to lock. 7. Press Power button to turn on the unit. 8. Then press Ice Cream button. 9. When the program is completed, turn the Outer Bowl and release it from the machine. 10. Transfer the ice cream into serving bowls and serve immediately.

French Vanilla Ice Cream

Prep time: 5 minutes | Cook time: 5 minutes | Serves 4

4 large egg yolks	⅓ cup whole milk
1 tablespoon light corn syrup	1 cup heavy (whipping) cream
¼ cup plus 1 tablespoon granulated sugar	1 teaspoon vanilla extract

1. Fill a large bowl with ice water and set it aside. 2. In a small saucepan, whisk together the egg yolks, corn syrup, and sugar until the mixture is fully combined and the sugar is dissolved. Do not do this over heat. 3. Whisk in the milk, heavy cream, and vanilla until combined. 4. Place the pan over medium heat. Cook, stirring constantly with a rubber spatula, until the temperature reaches 165°F to 175°F on an instant-read thermometer. 5. Remove the pan from the heat and pour the base through a fine-mesh strainer into a clean CREAMi Pint. Carefully place the container in the prepared ice water bath, making sure the water doesn't spill into the base. 6. Once the base has cooled, place the storage lid on the pint and freeze for 24 hours. 7. Remove the CREAMi Pint from the freezer and take off the lid. Place the pint in the outer bowl of your Ninja CREAMi, install the Creamerizer Paddle in the outer bowl lid, and lock the lid assembly onto the outer bowl. Place the bowl assembly on the motor base, and twist the handle to the right to raise the platform and lock it in place. Select the Ice Cream function. 8. Once the machine has finished processing, remove the ice cream from the pint. Serve immediately.

Mocha Ice Cream

Prep time: 5 minutes | Cook time: 5 minutes | Serves 4

½ cup mocha cappuccino mix	3 tablespoons agave nectar
1¾ cups coconut cream	

1. In a bowl, add all ingredients and beat until well combined. 2. Transfer the mixture into an empty Ninja CREAMi pint container. 3. Cover the container with storage lid and freeze for 24 hours. 4. After 24 hours, remove the lid from container and arrange into the Outer Bowl of Ninja CREAMi. 5. Install the Creamerizer Paddle onto the lid of Outer Bowl. 6. Then rotate the lid clockwise to lock. 7. Press Power button to turn on the unit. 8. Then press Ice Cream button. 9. When the program is completed, turn the Outer Bowl and release it from the machine. 10. Transfer the ice cream into serving bowls and serve immediately.

Fruity Carrot Ice Cream

Prep time: 5 minutes | Cook time: 5 minutes | Serves 4

¾ cup heavy cream	¾ cup sugar
½ cup milk	¼ cup frozen carrots
⅓ cup orange juice	¼ cup pineapple chunks

1. In a bowl, add the heavy cream, milk, orange juice and sugar and beat until well combined. 2. In an empty Ninja CREAMi pint container, place the carrots and pineapple chunks and top with milk mixture. 3. Cover the container with the storage lid and freeze for 24 hours. 4. After 24 hours, remove the lid from container and arrange into the outer bowl of Ninja CREAMi. 5. Install the "Creamerizer Paddle" onto the lid of outer bowl. 6. Then rotate the lid clockwise to lock. 7. Press "Power" button to turn on the unit. 8. Then press "ICE CREAM" button. 9. When the program is completed, turn the outer bowl and release it from the machine. 10. Transfer the ice cream into serving bowls and serve immediately.

Coconut-vanilla Ice Cream

Prep time: 5 minutes | Cook time: 5 minutes | Serves 4

1 can full-fat unsweetened coconut milk

½ cup organic sugar

1 teaspoon vanilla extract

1. In a large bowl, whisk together the coconut milk, sugar, and vanilla until everything is incorporated and the sugar is dissolved. 2. Pour the base into a clean CREAMi Pint. Place the storage lid on the container and freeze for 24 hours. 3. Remove the CREAMi Pint from the freezer and take off the lid. Place the pint in the outer bowl of your Ninja CREAMi, install the Creamerizer Paddle in the outer bowl lid, and lock the lid assembly onto the outer bowl. Place the bowl assembly on the motor base, and twist the handle to the right to raise the platform and lock it in place. Select the Ice Cream function. 4. Once the machine has finished processing, remove the ice cream from the pint. Serve immediately with desired toppings.

Pear Ice Cream

Prep time: 5 minutes | Cook time: 15 minutes | Serves 4

3 medium ripe pears, peeled, cored and cut into 1-inch pieces

1 can full-fat unsweetened coconut milk

½ cup granulated sugar

1. In a medium saucepan, add all ingredients and stir to combine. 2. Place the saucepan over medium heat and bring to a boil. 3. Reduce the heat to low and simmer for about ten minutes or until liquid is reduced by half. 4. Remove from the heat and set aside to cool. 5. After cooling, transfer the mixture into a high-speed blender and pulse until smooth. 6. Transfer the mixture into an empty Ninja CREAMi pint container. 7. Cover the container with storage lid and freeze for 24 hours. 8. After 24 hours, remove the lid from container and arrange into the Outer Bowl of Ninja CREAMi. 9. Install the Creamerizer Paddle onto the lid of Outer Bowl. 10. Then rotate the lid clockwise to lock. 11. Press Power button to turn on the unit. 12. Then press Ice Cream button. 13. When the program is completed, turn the Outer Bowl and release it from the machine. 14. Transfer the ice cream into serving bowls and serve immediately.

Chocolate Ice Cream

Prep time: 5 minutes | Cook time: 5 minutes | Serves 1

¾ cup heavy whipping cream

½ can sweetened condensed milk

½ cup unsweetened cocoa powder

½ teaspoon vanilla extract

1. In a medium mixing bowl, combine the sweetened condensed milk, cocoa powder, and vanilla extract. 2. In a separate bowl, whip the heavy cream until it forms firm peaks (do not overbeat). 3. Pour mixture into an empty ninja CREAMi Pint container and freeze for 24 hours. 4. After 24 hours, remove the Pint from the freezer. Remove the lid. 5. Place the Ninja CREAMi Pint into the outer bowl. Place the outer bowl with the Pint in it into the ninja CREAMi machine and turn until the outer bowl locks into place. Push the ICE CREAM button. During the ICE CREAM function, the ice cream will mix together and become very creamy. 6. Once the ICE CREAM function has ended, turn the outer bowl and release it from the ninja CREAMi machine.

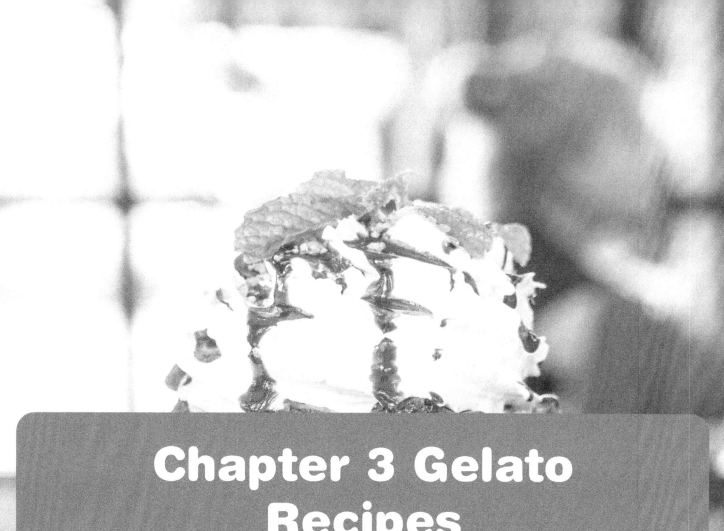

Chapter 3 Gelato Recipes

Chapter 3 Gelato Recipes

Cherry Gelato

Prep time: 6 minutes | Cook time: 3 minutes | Serves 4

4 large egg yolks
1 tablespoon light corn syrup
5 tablespoons granulated sugar
1 cup heavy cream

⅓ cup whole milk
1 teaspoon almond extract
1 cup frozen black cherries, pitted and quartered

1. In a small saucepan, add the egg yolks, sugar and corn syrup and beat until well combined. 2. Add the heavy cream, milk and almond extract and beat until well combined. 3. Place the saucepan over medium heat and cook for about 2-3 minutes, stirring continuously. 4. Remove from the heat and through a fine-mesh strainer, strain the mixture into an empty Ninja CREAMi pint container. 5. Place the container into an ice bath to cool. 6. After cooling, cover the container with the storage lid and freeze for 24 hours. 7. After 24 hours, remove the lid from container and arrange into the outer bowl of Ninja CREAMi. 8. Install the "Creamerizer Paddle" onto the lid of outer bowl. 9. Then rotate the lid clockwise to lock. 10. Press "Power" button to turn on the unit. 11. Then press "GELATO" button. 12. When the program is completed, with a spoon, create a 1½-inch wide hole in the center that reaches the bottom of the pint container. 13. Add the cherries into the hole and press "MIX-IN" button. 14. When the program is completed, turn the outer bowl and release it from the machine. 15. Transfer the gelato into serving bowls and serve immediately.

Cantaloupe Sorbet

Prep time: 5 minutes | Cook time: 10 minutes | Serves 4

3 cups cantaloupe pieces
⅓ cup water
⅓ cup organic sugar

1 tablespoon freshly squeezed lemon juice

1. Combine the cantaloupe, water, sugar, and lemon juice in a blender. Blend on high until smooth. 2. Pour the base into a clean CREAMi Pint. Place the storage lid on the container and freeze for 24 hours. 3. Remove the pint from the freezer and take off the lid. Place the pint in the outer bowl of your Ninja CREAMi, install the Creamerizer Paddle in the outer bowl lid, and lock the lid assembly onto the outer bowl. Place the bowl assembly on the motor base, and twist the handle to the right to raise the platform and lock it in place. Select the Sorbet function. 4. Once the machine has finished processing, remove the sorbet from the pint. Serve immediately.

Squash Gelato

Prep time: 5 minutes | Cook time: 5 minutes | Serves 4

1¾ cups milk
½ cup cooked butternut squash
¼ cup granulated sugar

½ teaspoon ground cinnamon
¼ teaspoon ground allspice
Pinch of salt

1. In a small saucepan, add all ingredients and beat until well combined. 2. Place the saucepan over medium heat and cook for about 5 minutes, stirring continuously. 3. Remove from the heat and transfer the mixture into an empty Ninja CREAMi pint container. 4. Place the container into an ice bath to cool. 5. After cooling, cover the container with the storage lid and freeze for 24 hours. 6. After 24 hours, remove the lid from container and arrange into the outer bowl of Ninja CREAMi. 7. Install the "Creamerizer Paddle" onto the lid of outer bowl. 8. Then rotate the lid clockwise to lock. 9. Press "Power" button to turn on the unit. 10. Then press "GELATO" button. 11. When the program is completed, turn the outer bowl and release it from the machine. 12. Transfer the gelato into serving bowls and serve immediately.

Chocolate Hazelnut Gelato

Prep time: 5 minutes | Cook time: 3 minutes | Serves 4

3 large egg yolks
⅓ cup hazelnut spread
¼ cup granulated sugar
2 teaspoons cocoa powder

1 tablespoon light corn syrup
1 cup whole milk
½ cup heavy cream
1 teaspoon vanilla extract

1. In a small saucepan, add the egg yolks, hazelnut spread, sugar, cocoa powder and corn syrup and beat until well combined. 2. Add the milk, heavy cream and vanilla extract and beat until well combined. 3. Place the saucepan over medium heat and cook for about 2-3 minutes, stirring continuously. 4. Remove from the heat and through a fine-mesh strainer, strain the mixture into an empty Ninja CREAMi pint container. 5. Place the container into an ice bath to cool. 6. After cooling, cover the container with the storage lid and freeze for 24 hours. 7. After 24 hours, remove the lid from container and arrange into the outer bowl of Ninja CREAMi. 8. Install the "Creamerizer Paddle" onto the lid of outer bowl. 9. Then rotate the lid clockwise to lock. 10. Press "Power" button to turn on the unit. 11. Then press "GELATO" button. 12. When the program is completed, turn the outer bowl and release it from the machine. 13. Transfer the gelato into serving bowls and serve immediately.

Blueberry & Crackers Gelato

Prep time: 10 minutes | Cook time: 3 minutes | Serves 4

4 large egg yolks	⅓ cup heavy cream
3 tablespoons granulated sugar	¼ cup cream cheese, softened
3 tablespoons wild blueberry preserves	3-6 drops purple food coloring
1 teaspoon vanilla extract	2 large graham crackers, broken in 1-inch pieces
1 cup whole milk	

1. In a small saucepan, add the egg yolks, sugar, blueberry preserves and vanilla extract and beat until well combined. 2. Add the milk, heavy cream, cream cheese and food coloring and beat until well combined. 3. Place the saucepan over medium heat and cook for about 2-3 minutes, stirring continuously. 4. Remove from the heat and through a fine-mesh strainer, strain the mixture into an empty Ninja CREAMi pint container. 5. Place the container into an ice bath to cool. 6. After cooling, cover the container with the storage lid and freeze for 24 hours. 7. After 24 hours, remove the lid from container and arrange into the outer bowl of Ninja CREAMi. 8. Install the "Creamerizer Paddle" onto the lid of outer bowl. 9. Then rotate the lid clockwise to lock. 10. Press "Power" button to turn on the unit. 11. Then press "GELATO" button. 12. When the program is completed, with a spoon, create a 1½-inch wide hole in the center that reaches the bottom of the pint container. 13. Add the graham crackers into the hole and press "MIX-IN" button. 14. When the program is completed, turn the outer bowl and release it from the machine. 15. Transfer the gelato into serving bowls and serve immediately.

White Chocolate-raspberry Gelato

Prep time: 10 minutes | Cook time: 10 minutes | Serves 4

1 cup whole milk, divided	⅓ cup, plus ¾ cup granulated sugar
1 tablespoon, plus ¼ cup cornstarch	
½ cup heavy (whipping) cream	½ cup raspberries
1 teaspoon vanilla extract	4 tablespoons water, divided
	¼ cup white chocolate chips

1. Fill a large bowl with ice water and set it aside. 2. In a small bowl, mix together ⅓ cup of milk and 1 tablespoon of cornstarch; set aside. 3. In a small saucepan, combine the remaining ⅔ cup of milk, the heavy cream, vanilla, and ⅓ cup of sugar. Whisk thoroughly to combine. 4. Place the pan over medium-high heat and bring the mixture to a simmer for about 4 minutes. Whisk in the cornstarch slurry and continue whisking constantly for about 1 minute. 5. Remove the pan from the heat and pour the base through a fine-mesh strainer into a clean CREAMi Pint. Carefully place the container in the prepared ice water bath, making sure the water doesn't spill into the base. 6. While the base chills, place the raspberries, remaining ¾ cup of sugar, and 2 tablespoons of water in a small saucepan. Place the pan over medium heat.

Cook, stirring constantly, for about 5 minutes, until the mixture is bubbling and the raspberries have broken down. 7. In a small bowl, whisk together the remaining 2 tablespoons of water and ¼ cup of cornstarch. Pour this mixture into the raspberry liquid. Continue to cook, stirring until the mixture has thickened, about 1 minute. Pour the raspberry mixture into a clean container, then carefully place the container in the ice water bath, making sure the water doesn't spill inside the container. 8. Once the base and raspberry mixtures are cold, carefully fold the raspberry mixture into the gelato base. Pour this mixture back into the CREAMi Pint, place the storage lid on the container, and freeze for 24 hours. 9. Remove the pint from the freezer and take off the lid. Place the pint in the outer bowl of your Ninja CREAMi, install the Creamerizer Paddle in the outer bowl lid, and lock the lid assembly onto the outer bowl. Place the bowl assembly on the motor base, and twist the handle to the right to raise the platform and lock it in place. Select the Gelato function. 10. Once the machine has finished processing, remove the lid from the pint. With a spoon, create a 1½-inch-wide hole that reaches the bottom of the pint. During this process, it is okay if your treat reaches above the Max Fill line. Add the white chocolate chips to the hole in the pint, replace the lid, and select the Mix-In function. 11. Once the machine has finished processing, remove the gelato from the pint. Serve immediately with desired toppings.

Pecan Gelato

Prep time: 10 minutes | Cook time: 3 minutes | Serves 4

4 large egg yolks	⅓ cup whole milk
5 tablespoons granulated sugar	1 teaspoon butter flavor extract
1 tablespoon light corn syrup	⅓ cup pecans, chopped
1 cup heavy cream	

1. In a small saucepan, add the egg yolks, sugar and corn syrup and beat until well combined. 2. Add the heavy cream, milk and butter flavor extract and beat until well combined. 3. Place the saucepan over medium heat and cook for about 2-3 minutes, stirring continuously. 4. Remove from the heat and through a fine-mesh strainer, strain the mixture into an empty Ninja CREAMi pint container. 5. Place the container into an ice bath to cool. 6. After cooling, cover the container with the storage lid and freeze for 24 hours. 7. After 24 hours, remove the lid from container and arrange into the outer bowl of Ninja CREAMi. 8. Install the "Creamerizer Paddle" onto the lid of outer bowl. 9. Then rotate the lid clockwise to lock. 10. Press "Power" button to turn on the unit. 11. Then press "GELATO" button. 12. When the program is completed, with a spoon, create a 1½-inch wide hole in the center that reaches the bottom of the pint container. 13. Add the pecans into the hole and press "MIX-IN" button. 14. When the program is completed, turn the outer bowl and release it from the machine. 15. Transfer the gelato into serving bowls and serve immediately.

Banana & Squash Cookie Gelato

Prep time: 5 minutes | Cook time: 3 minutes | Serves 4

4 large egg yolks	chopped
1 cup heavy cream	1 box instant vanilla pudding
⅓ cup granulated sugar	mix
½ of banana, peeled and sliced	6 vanilla wafer cookies,
½ cup frozen butternut squash,	crumbled

1. In a small saucepan, add the egg yolks, heavy cream and sugar and beat until well combined. 2. Place the saucepan over medium heat and cook for about 2-3 minutes, stirring continuously. 3. Remove from the heat and through a fine-mesh strainer, strain the mixture into an empty Ninja CREAMi pint container. 4. Place the container into an ice bath to cool. 5. After cooling, add in the banana, squash and pudding until well combined. 6. Cover the container with the storage lid and freeze for 24 hours. 7. After 24 hours, remove the lid from container and arrange into the outer bowl of Ninja CREAMi. 8. Install the "Creamerizer Paddle" onto the lid of outer bowl. 9. Then rotate the lid clockwise to lock. 10. Press "Power" button to turn on the unit. 11. Then press "GELATO" button. 12. When the program is completed, with a spoon, create a 1½-inch wide hole in the center that reaches the bottom of the pint container. 13. Add the wafer cookies into the hole and press "MIX-IN" button. 14. When the program is completed, turn the outer bowl and release it from the machine. 15. Transfer the gelato into serving bowls and serve immediately.

Vanilla Gelato

Prep time: 5 minutes | Cook time: 3 minutes | Serves 4

4 large egg yolks	1 cup heavy cream
1 tablespoon light corn syrup	⅓ cup whole milk
¼ cup plus 1 tablespoon	1 whole vanilla bean, split in
granulated sugar	half lengthwise and scraped

1. In a small saucepan, add the egg yolks, corn syrup and sugar and beat until well combined. 2. Add the heavy cream, milk and vanilla bean and beat until well combined. 3. Place the saucepan over medium heat and cook for about 2-3 minutes, stirring continuously. 4. Remove from the heat and through a fine-mesh strainer, strain the mixture into an empty Ninja CREAMi pint container. 5. Place the container into an ice bath to cool. 6. After cooling, cover the container with the storage lid and freeze for 24 hours. 7. After 24 hours, remove the lid from container and arrange into the outer bowl of Ninja CREAMi. 8. Install the "Creamerizer Paddle" onto the lid of outer bowl. 9. Then rotate the lid clockwise to lock. 10. Press "Power" button to turn on the unit. 11. Then press "GELATO" button. 12. When the program is completed, turn the outer bowl and release it from the machine. 13. Transfer the gelato into serving bowls and serve immediately.

Carrot Gelato

Prep time: 5 minutes | Cook time: 3 minutes | Serves 4

3 large egg yolks	½ cup carrot puree
⅓ cup coconut sugar	½ teaspoon ground cinnamon
1 tablespoon brown rice syrup	¼ teaspoon ground nutmeg
½ cup heavy cream	¼ teaspoon ground ginger
1 cup unsweetened almond	¼ teaspoon ground cloves
milk	¾ teaspoon vanilla extract

1. In a small saucepan, add the egg yolks, coconut sugar and brown rice syrup and beat until well combined. 2. Add the heavy cream, almond milk, carrot puree and spices and beat until well combined. 3. Place the saucepan over medium heat and cook for about 2-3 minutes, stirring continuously. 4. Remove from the heat and stir in the vanilla extract. 5. Through a fine-mesh strainer, strain the mixture into an empty Ninja CREAMi pint container. 6. Place the container into an ice bath to cool. 7. After cooling, cover the container with the storage lid and freeze for 24 hours. 8. After 24 hours, remove the lid from container and arrange into the outer bowl of Ninja CREAMi. 9. Install the "Creamerizer Paddle" onto the lid of outer bowl. 10. Then rotate the lid clockwise to lock. 11. Press "Power" button to turn on the unit. 12. Then press "GELATO" button. 13. When the program is completed, turn the outer bowl and release it from the machine. 14. Transfer the gelato into serving bowls and serve immediately.

Maple Gelato

Prep time: 5 minutes | Cook time: 3 minutes | Serves 4

4 large egg yolks	1 teaspoon maple extract
½ cup plus 1 tablespoon light	1 cup whole milk
brown sugar	⅓ cup heavy cream
1 tablespoon maple syrup	

1. In a small saucepan, add the egg yolks, brown sugar, maple syrup and maple extract and beat until well combined. 2. Add the milk and heavy cream and beat until well combined. 3. Place the saucepan over medium heat and cook for about 2-3 minutes, stirring continuously. 4. Remove from the heat and through a fine-mesh strainer, strain the mixture into an empty Ninja CREAMi pint container. 5. Place the container into an ice bath to cool. 6. After cooling, cover the container with the storage lid and freeze for 24 hours. 7. After 24 hours, remove the lid from container and arrange into the outer bowl of Ninja CREAMi. 8. Install the "Creamerizer Paddle" onto the lid of outer bowl. 9. Then rotate the lid clockwise to lock. 10. Press "Power" button to turn on the unit. 11. Then press "GELATO" button. 12. When the program is completed, turn the outer bowl and release it from the machine. Transfer the gelato into serving bowls and serve immediately.

Berries Mascarpone Gelato

Prep time: 5 minutes | Cook time: 3 minutes | Serves 4

3 large egg yolks	¾ cup whole milk
½ cup plus 2 tablespoons granulated sugar, divided	¼ cup heavy cream
1 tablespoon light corn syrup	½ teaspoon vanilla extract
½ cup mascarpone	1 cup frozen mixed berries

1. In a small saucepan, add the egg yolks, ½ cup of sugar and corn syrup and beat until well combined. 2. Add the mascarpone milk, heavy cream and vanilla extract and beat until well combined. 3. Place the saucepan over medium heat and cook for about 2-3 minutes, stirring continuously. 4. Remove from the heat and through a fine-mesh strainer, strain the mixture into an empty Ninja CREAMi pint container. 5. Place the container into an ice bath to cool. 6. After cooling, cover the container with the storage lid and freeze for 24 hours. 7. Meanwhile, in a small saucepan, add the mixed berries and remaining sugar over medium heat and cook for about 8 minutes, stirring occasionally and mashing to form a thick jam. 8. Remove from heat and transfer the jam into a bowl. 9. Refrigerate the jam until using. 10. After 24 hours, remove the lid from container and arrange the container into the outer bowl of Ninja CREAMi. 11. Install the "Creamerizer Paddle" onto the lid of outer bowl. 12. Then rotate the lid clockwise to lock. 13. Press "Power" button to turn on the unit. 14. Then press "GELATO" button. 15. When the program is completed, with a spoon, create a 1½-inch wide hole in the center that reaches the bottom of the pint container. 16. Add the berry jam into the hole and press "MIX-IN" button. 17. When the program is completed, turn the outer bowl and release it from the machine. 18. Transfer the gelato into serving bowls and serve immediately.

Peanut Butter Gelato

Prep time: 20 minutes | Cook time: 10 minutes | Serves 4

1½ Cups unsweetened coconut milk	3 tablespoons peanut butter
6 tablespoons sugar	3 dark chocolate peanut butter Cups, cut each into 8 pieces
1 tablespoon cornstarch	2 tablespoons peanuts, chopped

1. In a small saucepan, add the coconut milk, sugar, and cornstarch and mix well. 2. Place the saucepan over medium heat and bring to a boil, beating continuously. 3. Reduce the heat to low and simmer for about 3-4 minutes. 4. Remove from the heat and stir in the peanut butter. 5. Transfer the mixture into an empty Ninja CREAMi pint container. 6. Place the container into an ice bath to cool. 7. After cooling, cover the container with the storage lid and freeze for 24 hours. 8. After 24 hours, remove the lid from container and arrange into the outer bowl of Ninja CREAMi. 9. Install the "Creamerizer Paddle" onto the lid of outer bowl. 10. Then rotate the lid clockwise to lock. 11. Press "Power" button to turn on the unit. 12. Then press "GELATO" button. 13. When the program is completed, with a spoon, create a 1½-inch wide hole in the center that reaches the bottom of the pint container. 14. Add the peanut butter Cup and peanuts into the hole and press "MIX-IN" button. 15. When the program is completed, turn the outer bowl and release it from the machine. 16. Transfer the gelato into serving bowls and serve immediately.

Apple Cider Sorbet

Prep time: 5 minutes | Cook time: 3 minutes | Serves 4

1 cup apple cider	2 tablespoons organic sugar
1 cup applesauce	

1. In a large bowl, whisk together the apple cider, applesauce, and sugar until the sugar is dissolved. 2. Pour the base into a clean CREAMi Pint. Place the storage lid on the container and freeze for 24 hours. 3. Remove the pint from the freezer and take off the lid. Place the pint in the outer bowl of your Ninja CREAMi, install the Creamerizer Paddle in the outer bowl lid, and lock the lid assembly onto the outer bowl. Place the bowl assembly on the motor base, and twist the handle to the right to raise the platform and lock it in place. Select the Sorbet function. 4. Once the machine has finished processing, remove the sorbet from the pint. Serve immediately.

Triple Chocolate Gelato

Prep time: 5 minutes | Cook time: 3 minutes | Serves 4

4 large egg yolks	topping
⅓ cup dark brown sugar	¾ cup heavy cream
2 tablespoons dark cocoa powder	¾ cup whole milk
1 tablespoon chocolate fudge	2-3 tablespoons chocolate chunks, chopped

1. In a small saucepan, add the egg yolks, sugar, cocoa powder and chocolate fudge and beat until well combined. 2. Add the heavy cream and milk and beat until well combined. 3. Place the saucepan over medium heat and cook for about 2-3 minutes, stirring continuously. 4. Remove from the heat and stir in chocolate chunks until melted completely. 5. Through a fine-mesh strainer, strain the mixture into an empty Ninja CREAMi pint container. 6. Place the container into an ice bath to cool. 7. After cooling, cover the container with the storage lid and freeze for 24 hours. 8. After 24 hours, remove the lid from container and arrange into the outer bowl of Ninja CREAMi. 9. Install the "Creamerizer Paddle" onto the lid of outer bowl. 10. Then rotate the lid clockwise to lock. 11. Press "Power" button to turn on the unit. 12. Then press "GELATO" button. 13. When the program is completed, turn the outer bowl and release it from the machine. 14. Transfer the gelato into serving bowls and serve immediately.

Spirulina Cookie Gelato

Prep time: 5 minutes | Cook time: 3 minutes | Serves 4

4 large egg yolks	1 teaspoon blue spirulina
⅓ cup granulated sugar	powder
1 up oat milk	4 small crunchy chocolate chip
1 teaspoon vanilla extract	cookies, crumbled

1. In a small saucepan, add the egg yolks and sugar and beat until well combined. 2. Add oat milk and vanilla extract and stir to combine. 3. Place the saucepan over medium heat and cook for about 2-3 minutes, stirring continuously. 4. Remove from the heat and through a fine-mesh strainer, strain the mixture into an empty Ninja CREAMi pint container. 5. Place the container into an ice bath to cool. 6. After cooling, cover the container with the storage lid and freeze for 24 hours. 7. After 24 hours, remove the lid from container and arrange into the outer bowl of Ninja CREAMi. 8. Install the "Creamerizer Paddle" onto the lid of outer bowl. 9. Then rotate the lid clockwise to lock. 10. Press "Power" button to turn on the unit. 11. Then press "GELATO" button. 12. When the program is completed, with a spoon, create a 1½-inch wide hole in the center that reaches the bottom of the pint container. 13. Add the chocolate chip cookies into the hole and press "MIX-IN" button. 14. When the program is completed, turn the outer bowl and release it from the machine. 15. Transfer the gelato into serving bowls and serve immediately.

Pumpkin Gelato

Prep time: 5 minutes | Cook time: 3 minutes | Serves 4

3 large egg yolks	½ cup canned pumpkin puree
⅓ cup granulated sugar	1½ teaspoons pumpkin pie
1 tablespoon light corn syrup	spice
1 cup whole milk	1 teaspoon vanilla extract
½ cup heavy cream	

1. In a small saucepan, add the egg yolks, sugar and corn syrup and beat until well combined. 2. Add the milk, heavy cream, pumpkin puree and pumpkin pie spice and beat until well combined. 3. Place the saucepan over medium heat and cook for about 2-3 minutes, stirring continuously. 4. Remove from the heat and stir in the vanilla extract. 5. Through a fine-mesh strainer, strain the mixture into an empty Ninja CREAMi pint container. 6. Place the container into an ice bath to cool. 7. After cooling, cover the container with the storage lid and freeze for 24 hours. 8. After 24 hours, remove the lid from container and arrange into the outer bowl of Ninja CREAMi. 9. Install the "Creamerizer Paddle" onto the lid of outer bowl. 10. Then rotate the lid clockwise to lock. 11. Press "Power" button to turn on the unit. 12. Then press "GELATO" button. 13. When the program is completed, turn the outer bowl and release it from the machine. 14. Transfer the gelato into serving bowls and serve immediately.

Sweet Potato Gelato

Prep time: 5 minutes | Cook time: 3 minutes | Serves 4

½ cup canned sweet potato	½ teaspoon ground cinnamon
puree	⅛ teaspoon ground nutmeg
4 large egg yolks	1 cup heavy cream
¼ cup sugar	1 teaspoon vanilla extract

1. In a small saucepan, add the sweet potato puree, egg yolks, sugar, ½ teaspoon of cinnamon and nutmeg and beat until well combined. 2. Add the heavy cream and vanilla extract and beat until well combined. 3. Place the saucepan over medium heat and cook for about 2-3 minutes, stirring continuously. 4. Remove from the heat and through a fine-mesh strainer, strain the mixture into an empty Ninja CREAMi pint container. 5. Place the container into an ice bath to cool. 6. After cooling, cover the container with the storage lid and freeze for 24 hours. 7. After 24 hours, remove the lid from container and arrange into the outer bowl of Ninja CREAMi. 8. Install the "Creamerizer Paddle" onto the lid of outer bowl. 9. Then rotate the lid clockwise to lock. 10. Press "Power" button to turn on the unit. 11. Then press "GELATO" button. 12. When the program is completed, turn the outer bowl and release it from the machine. 13. Transfer the gelato into serving bowls and serve immediately.

Vanilla Bean Gelato

Prep time: 5 minutes | Cook time: 3 minutes | Serves 4

4 large egg yolks	⅓ cup whole milk
1 tablespoon light corn syrup	1 cup heavy (whipping) cream
¼ cup plus 1 tablespoon	1 whole vanilla bean, split in
granulated sugar	half lengthwise and scraped

1. Fill a large bowl with ice water and set it aside. 2. In a small saucepan, whisk together the egg yolks, corn syrup, and sugar until everything is fully combined and the sugar is dissolved. Do not do this over heat. 3. Whisk in the milk, heavy cream, and vanilla bean scrapings (discard the pod). 4. Place the pan over medium heat. Cook, stirring constantly with a rubber spatula, until the temperature reaches 165°F to 175°F on an instant-read thermometer. 5. Remove the pan from the heat and pour the base through a fine-mesh strainer into a clean CREAMi Pint. Carefully place the container in the prepared ice water bath, making sure the water doesn't spill into the base. 6. Once the base has cooled, place the storage lid on the pint and freeze for 24 hours. 7. Remove the pint from the freezer and take off the lid. Place the pint in the outer bowl of your Ninja CREAMi, install the Creamerizer Paddle in the outer bowl lid, and lock the lid assembly onto the outer bowl. Place the bowl assembly on the motor base, and twist the handle to the right to raise the platform and lock it in place. Select the Gelato function. 8. Once the machine has finished processing, remove the gelato from the pint. Serve immediately with desired toppings.

Pistachio Gelato

Prep time: 5 minutes | Cook time: 3 minutes | Serves 4

4 large egg yolks	1 cup heavy (whipping) cream
¼ cup plus 1 tablespoon granulated sugar	1 teaspoon almond extract
1 tablespoon light corn syrup	5 drops green food coloring
⅓ cup whole milk	¼ cup roasted pistachios

1. Fill a large bowl with ice water and set it aside. 2. In a small saucepan, whisk together the egg yolks, sugar, and corn syrup until the mixture is fully combined and the sugar is dissolved. Do not do this over heat. 3. Whisk in the milk, heavy cream, almond extract, and food coloring. 4. Place the pan over medium heat. Cook, stirring constantly with a rubber spatula, until the temperature reaches 165°F to 175°F on an instant-read thermometer. 5. Remove the pan from the heat and pour the base through a fine-mesh strainer into a clean CREAMi Pint. Carefully place the container in the prepared ice water bath, making sure the water doesn't spill into the base. 6. Once the base has cooled, place the storage lid on the pint and freeze for 24 hours. 7. Remove the pint from the freezer and take off the lid. Place the pint in the outer bowl of your Ninja CREAMi, install the Creamerizer Paddle in the outer bowl lid, and lock the lid assembly onto the outer bowl. Place the bowl assembly on the motor base, and twist the handle to the right to raise the platform and lock it in place. Select the Gelato function. 8. Once the machine has finished processing, remove the lid from the pint container. With a spoon, create a 1½-inch-wide hole that reaches the bottom of the pint. During this process, it is okay if your treat reaches above the Max Fill line. Add the pistachios to the hole in the pint, replace the lid, and select the Mix-In function. 9. Once the machine has finished processing, remove the gelato from the pint. Serve immediately.

Strawberry Cheesecake Gelato

Prep time: 5 minutes | Cook time: 8 minutes | Serves 4

4 large egg yolks	temperature
3 tablespoons granulated sugar	1 teaspoon vanilla extract
1 cup whole milk	3 tablespoons strawberry jam
⅓ cup heavy (whipping) cream	¼ cup graham cracker pieces
¼ cup cream cheese, at room	

1. Fill a large bowl with ice water and set it aside. 2. In a small saucepan, whisk together the egg yolks and sugar until the mixture is smooth and the sugar is dissolved. Do not do this over heat. 3. Whisk in the milk, heavy cream, cream cheese, vanilla, and strawberry jam. 4. Place the pan over medium heat. Cook, stirring constantly with a rubber spatula, until the temperature reaches 165°F to 175°F on an instant-read thermometer. 5. Remove the pan from the heat and pour the base through a fine-mesh strainer into a clean CREAMi Pint. Carefully place the container in the prepared ice water bath, making sure the water doesn't spill into the base. 6. Once the base has cooled, place the storage lid on the pint and freeze for 24 hours. 7. Remove the pint from the freezer and take off the lid. Place the pint in the outer bowl of your Ninja CREAMi, install the Creamerizer Paddle in the outer bowl lid, and lock the lid assembly onto the outer bowl. Place the bowl assembly on the motor base, and twist the handle to the right to raise the platform and lock it in place. Select the Gelato function. 8. Once the machine has finished processing, remove the lid from the pint container. With a spoon, create a 1½-inch-wide hole that reaches the bottom of the pint. During this process, it is okay if your treat reaches above the Max Fill line. Add the graham cracker pieces to the hole in the pint, replace the lid, and select the Mix-In function. 9. Once the machine has finished processing, remove the gelato from the pint. Serve immediately.

Marshmallow Gelato

Prep time: 20 minutes | Cook time: 5 minutes | Serves 4

1 cup whole milk	3 egg yolk
½ cup heavy cream	Pinch of sea salt
¼ cup sugar	¼ cup mini marshmallows

1. Preheat the oven to broiler. Lightly grease a baking sheet. 2. Arrange the marshmallows onto the prepared baking sheet in a single layer. 3. Broil for about 5 minutes, flipping once halfway through. 4. Meanwhile, in a small saucepan, add the milk, heavy cream, sugar, egg yolks and a pinch of salt and beat until well combined. 5. Place the saucepan over medium heat and cook for about 1 minute, stirring continuously. 6. Remove from the heat and stir in half of the marshmallows. 7. Transfer the mixture into an empty Ninja CREAMi pint container. 8. Place the container into an ice bath to cool. 9. After cooling, cover the container with the storage lid and freeze for 24 hours. 10. Reserve the remaining marshmallows into the freezer. 11. After 24 hours, remove the lid from container and arrange into the outer bowl of Ninja CREAMi. 12. Install the "Creamerizer Paddle" onto the lid of outer bowl. 13. Then rotate the lid clockwise to lock. 14. Press "Power" button to turn on the unit. 15. Then press "GELATO" button. 16. When the program is completed, with a spoon, create a 1½-inch wide hole in the center that reaches the bottom of the pint container. 17. Add the reserved frozen marshmallows into the hole and press "MIX-IN" button. 18. When the program is completed, turn the outer bowl and release it from the machine. 19. Transfer the gelato into serving bowls and serve immediately.

Caramel Egg Gelato

Prep time: 15 minutes | Cook time: 10 minutes | Serves 4

¼ cup agave nectar

¾ cup unsweetened soy milk

½ cup unsweetened creamer

2 eggs

3 tablespoons granulated sugar

¼ cup caramels, chopped

1. In a medium saucepan, add agave nectar over medium-high heat and cook for about 2-3 minutes. 2. Remove the saucepan from heat and slowly whisk in the soy milk and creamer. 3. Return the pan over medium-high heat and whisk in the eggs and sugar. 4. Cook for about 4-5 minutes, stirring frequently. 5. Remove from the heat and through a fine-mesh strainer, strain the mixture into an empty Ninja CREAMi pint container. 6. Place the container into an ice bath to cool. 7. After cooling, cover the container with the storage lid and freeze for 24 hours. 8. After 24 hours, remove the lid from container and arrange into the outer bowl of Ninja CREAMi. 9. Install the "Creamerizer Paddle" onto the lid of outer bowl. 10. Then rotate the lid clockwise to lock. 11. Press "Power" button to turn on the unit. 12. Then press "GELATO" button. 13. When the program is completed, with a spoon, create a 1½-inch wide hole in the center that reaches the bottom of the pint container. 14. Add the chopped caramels into the hole and press "MIX-IN" button. 15. When the program is completed, turn the outer bowl and release it from the machine. 16. Transfer the gelato into serving bowls and serve immediately.

Marshmallow Cookie Gelato

Prep time: 5 minutes | Cook time: 6 minutes | Serves 4

1 whole vanilla bean, split in half lengthwise, scraped

4 egg yolks

¾ cup heavy cream

⅓ cup whole milk

2 tablespoons granulated sugar

1 tablespoon light corn syrup

1 teaspoon vanilla extract

5 tablespoons marshmallow paste

5 peanut butter cookies, chopped

1. In a medium saucepan, add the vanilla bean over medium-high heat, and toast for about 2-3 minutes, stirring continuously. 2. Reduce the heat to medium-low and whisk in the egg yolks, heavy cream, milk, sugar, corn syrup and vanilla extract. 3. Cook for about 2-3 minutes, stirring continuously. 4. Remove from the heat and through a fine-mesh strainer, strain the mixture into an empty Ninja CREAMi pint container. 5. Place the container into an ice bath to cool. 6. After cooling, cover the container with the storage lid and freeze for 24 hours. 7. After 24 hours, remove the lid from container and arrange into the outer bowl of Ninja CREAMi. 8. Install the "Creamerizer Paddle" onto the lid of outer bowl. 9. Then rotate the lid clockwise to lock. 10. Press "Power" button to turn on the unit. 11. Then press "GELATO" button. 12. When the program is completed, with a spoon, create a 1½-inch wide hole in the center that reaches the bottom of the pint container. 13. Add the cookies

into the hole and press "MIX-IN" button. 14. When the program is completed, turn the outer bowl and release it from the machine. 15. Transfer the gelato into serving bowls and serve immediately.

Red Velvet Gelato

Prep time: 5 minutes | Cook time: 3 minutes | Serves 4

4 large egg yolks

¼ cup granulated sugar

2 tablespoons unsweetened cocoa powder

1 cup whole milk

⅓ cup heavy (whipping) cream

¼ cup cream cheese, at room temperature

1 teaspoon vanilla extract

1 teaspoon red food coloring

1. Fill a large bowl with ice water and set it aside. 2. In a small saucepan, whisk together the egg yolks, sugar, and cocoa powder until everything is fully combined and the sugar is dissolved. Do not do this over heat. 3. Whisk in the milk, heavy cream, cream cheese, vanilla, and food coloring. 4. Place the pan over medium heat. Cook, stirring constantly with a rubber spatula, until the temperature reaches 165°F to 175°F on an instant-read thermometer. 5. Remove the pan from the heat and pour the base through a fine-mesh strainer into a clean CREAMi Pint. Carefully place the container in the prepared ice water bath, making sure the water doesn't spill into the base. 6. Once the base has cooled, place the storage lid on the pint and freeze for 24 hours. 7. Remove the pint from the freezer and take off the lid. Place the pint in the outer bowl of your Ninja CREAMi, install the Creamerizer Paddle in the outer bowl lid, and lock the lid assembly onto the outer bowl. Place the bowl assembly on the motor base, and twist the handle to the right to raise the platform and lock it in place. Select the Gelato function. 8. Once the machine has finished processing, remove the gelato from the pint. Serve immediately.

Orange Sherbet

Prep time: 5 minutes | Cook time: 3 minutes | Serves 4

1 cup orange juice

¼ cup plus 1 tablespoon granulated sugar

¼ cup whole milk

½ cup heavy (whipping) cream

1. In a large bowl, whisk together the orange juice, sugar, milk, and heavy cream until everything is well combined and the sugar is dissolved. 2. Pour the base into a clean CREAMi Pint. Place the storage lid on the container and freeze for 24 hours. 3. Remove the pint from the freezer and take off the lid. Place the pint in the outer bowl of your Ninja CREAMi, install the Creamerizer Paddle in the outer bowl lid, and lock the lid assembly onto the outer bowl. Place the bowl assembly on the motor base, and twist the handle to the right to raise the platform and lock it in place. Select the Ice Cream function. 4. Once the machine has finished processing, remove the sherbet from the pint. Serve immediately with desired toppings.

Chocolate Cauliflower Gelato

Prep time: 15 minutes | Cook time: 3 minutes | Serves 4

1 cup whole milk

½ cup heavy cream

⅓ cup sugar

2 tablespoons cocoa powder

½ cup frozen cauliflower rice

¼ teaspoon almond extract

Pinch of salt

½ cup dark chocolate, chopped

1. In a small saucepan, add all ingredients except for chopped chocolate and beat until well combined. 2. Place the saucepan over medium heat and cook for about 2-3 minutes, stirring continuously. 3. Remove from the heat and transfer the mixture into an empty Ninja CREAMi pint container. 4. Place the container into an ice bath to cool. 5. After cooling, cover the container with the storage lid and freeze for 24 hours. 6. After 24 hours, remove the lid from container and arrange into the outer bowl of Ninja CREAMi. 7. Install the "Creamerizer Paddle" onto the lid of outer bowl. 8. Then rotate the lid clockwise to lock. 9. Press "Power" button to turn on the unit. 10. Then press "GELATO" button. 11. When the program is completed, with a spoon, create a 1½-inch wide hole in the center that reaches the bottom of the pint container. 12. Add the chopped chocolate into the hole and press "MIX-IN" button. 13. When the program is completed, turn the outer bowl and release it from the machine. 14. Transfer the gelato into serving bowls and serve immediately.

Tiramisu Gelato

Prep time: 15 minutes | Cook time: 6 minutes | Serves 4

4 large egg yolks

⅓ cup granulated sugar

1 cup whole milk

⅓ cup heavy (whipping) cream

¼ cup cream cheese

1 tablespoon instant coffee

1 teaspoon rum extract

¼ cup ladyfinger pieces

1. Fill a large bowl with ice water and set it aside. 2. In a small saucepan, whisk together the egg yolks and sugar until the mixture is fully combined and the sugar is dissolved. Do not do this over heat. 3. Whisk in the milk, heavy cream, cream cheese, instant coffee, and rum extract. 4. Place the pan over medium heat. Cook, stirring constantly with a rubber spatula, until the temperature reaches 165°F to 175°F on an instant-read thermometer. 5. Remove the pan from the heat and pour the base through a fine-mesh strainer into a clean CREAMi Pint. Carefully place the container in the prepared ice water bath, making sure the water doesn't spill into the base. 6. Once the base has cooled, place the storage lid on the pint and freeze for 24 hours. 7. Remove the pint from the freezer and take off the lid. Place the pint in the outer bowl of your Ninja CREAMi, install the Creamerizer Paddle in the outer bowl lid, and lock the lid assembly onto the outer bowl. Place the bowl assembly on the motor base, and twist the handle to the right to raise the platform and lock it in place. Select the Gelato function. 8. Once the machine has finished processing, remove the lid from the pint container. With a spoon, create a 1½-inch-wide hole that reaches the bottom of the pint. During this process, it is okay if your treat reaches above the Max Fill line. Add the ladyfinger pieces to the hole in the pint, replace the lid, and select the Mix-In function. 9. Once the machine has finished processing, remove the gelato from the pint. Serve immediately.

Chapter 4 Smoothie Bowls Recipes

Chapter 4 Smoothie Bowls Recipes

Berries & Cherry Smoothie Bowl

Prep time: 5 minutes | Cook time: 5 minutes | Serves 4

1 cup cranberry juice cocktail	2 cups frozen cherry berry
¼ cup agave nectar	blend

1. In a large bowl, add the agave nectar and cranberry juice cocktail and beat until well combined. 2. Place the cherry berry blend into an empty Ninja CREAMi pint container. 3. Top with cocktail mixture and stir to combine. 4. Cover the container with storage lid and freeze for 24 hours. 5. After 24 hours, remove the lid from container and arrange into the Outer Bowl of Ninja CREAMi. 6. Install the Creamerizer Paddle onto the lid of outer bowl. 7. Then rotate the lid clockwise to lock. 8. Press Power button to turn on the unit. 9. Then press Smoothie Bowl button. 10. When the program is completed, turn the Outer Bowl and release it from the machine. 11. Transfer the smoothie into serving bowls and serve immediately.

Strawberry Smoothie Bowl

Prep time: 5 minutes | Cook time: 5 minutes | Serves 4

2 tablespoons vanilla protein powder	1 cup ripe banana, peeled and cut in ½-inch pieces
¼ cup agave nectar	1 cup fresh strawberries, hulled and quartered
¼ cup pineapple juice	
½ cup whole milk	

1. In a large bowl, add the protein powder, agave nectar, pineapple juice and milk and beat until well combined. 2. Place the banana and strawberry into an empty Ninja CREAMi pint container and with the back of a spoon, firmly press the fruit below the Max Fill line. 3. Top with milk mixture and mix until well combined. 4. Cover the container with storage lid and freeze for 24 hours. 5. After 24 hours, remove the lid from container and arrange into the Outer Bowl of Ninja CREAMi. 6. Install the Creamerizer Paddle onto the lid of Outer Bowl. 7. Then rotate the lid clockwise to lock. 8. Press Power button to turn on the unit. 9. Then press Smoothie Bowl button. 10. When the program is completed, turn the Outer Bowl and release it from the machine. 11. Transfer the smoothie into serving bowls and serve immediately.

Three Fruit Smoothie Bowl

Prep time: 5 minutes | Cook time: 3 minutes | Serves 2

1 cup frozen dragon fruit pieces	pieces
¾ cup fresh strawberries, hulled and quartered	½ cup low-fat plain yogurt
¾ cup pineapple, cut in 1-inch	2 tablespoons agave nectar
	1 tablespoon fresh lime juice

1. In a large high-speed blender, add all the ingredients and pulse until smooth. 2. Transfer the mixture into an empty Ninja CREAMi pint container. 3. Cover the container with the storage lid and freeze for 24 hours. 4. After 24 hours, remove the lid from container and arrange into the outer bowl of Ninja CREAMi. 5. Install the "Creamerizer Paddle" onto the lid of outer bowl. 6. Then rotate the lid clockwise to lock. 7. Press "Power" button to turn on the unit. 8. Then press "SMOOTHIE BOWL" button. 9. When the program is completed, turn the outer bowl and release it from the machine. 10. Transfer the smoothie into serving bowls and serve immediately.

Chocolate Pumpkin Smoothie Bowl

Prep time: 5 minutes | Cook time: 3 minutes | Serves 4

½ cup canned pumpkin puree	2 ripe bananas, cut in ½-inch
2 tablespoons unsweetened cocoa powder	pieces
	1 tablespoon agave nectar
1 teaspoon pumpkin spice seasoning	¼ cup whole milk

1. In a small bowl, stir together the pumpkin puree, cocoa powder, and pumpkin spice until well combined. Pour the base into a clean CREAMi Pint. Mix in the bananas, agave, and milk until everything is fully combined and the bananas are coated. Place the storage lid on the container and freeze for 24 hours. 2. Remove the pint from the freezer and take off the lid. Place the pint in the outer bowl of your Ninja CREAMi, install the Creamerizer Paddle in the outer bowl lid, and lock the lid assembly onto the outer bowl. Place the bowl assembly on the motor base, and twist the handle to the right to raise the platform and lock it in place. Select the Smoothie Bowl function. 3. Once the machine has finished processing, remove the smoothie bowl from the pint. Serve immediately with your desired toppings.

Crazy Fruit Smoothie

Prep time: 5 minutes | Cook time: 10 minutes | Serves 1

1 cup crushed ice	½ cup chopped pineapple
1 banana, chopped	¼ cup cream of coconut
1 kiwi, peeled and chopped	1 tablespoon coconut flakes, for
½ cup chopped strawberries	garnish

1. Add the ice, banana, kiwi, strawberries, pineapple, and cream of coconut into an empty ninja CREAMi Pint 2. Place the Ninja CREAMi Pint into the outer bowl. Place the outer bowl with the Pint in it into the ninja CREAMi machine and turn until the outer bowl locks into place. Push the SMOOTHIE button. During the SMOOTHIE function, the ingredients will mix together and become very creamy. 3. Once the SMOOTHIE function has ended, turn the outer bowl and release it from the ninja CREAMi machine. 4. Pour the smoothie into a tall glass.

Strawberry-orange Creme Smoothie

Prep time: 5 minutes | Cook time: 5 minutes | Serves 1

1 container Yoplait Greek 100	¼ cup ice cubes (optional)
orange creme yogurt	¼ cup orange juice
½ cup fresh strawberries, hulled	

1. Put all the ingredients into an empty ninja CREAMi Pint. 2. Place the Ninja CREAMi Pint into the outer bowl. Place the outer bowl with the Pint in it into the ninja CREAMi machine and turn until the outer bowl locks into place. Push the SMOOTHIE button. During the SMOOTHIE function, the ingredients will mix together and become very creamy. 3. Once the SMOOTHIE function has ended, turn the outer bowl and release it from the ninja CREAMi machine. 4. Scoop the smoothie into a tall glass.

Mango Smoothie Bowl

Prep time: 5 minutes | Cook time: 5 minutes | Serves 4

2 cups ripe mango, peeled, pitted and cut into 1-inch pieces
1 can of unsweetened coconut milk

1. Place the mango pieces into an empty Ninja CREAMi pint container. 2. Top with coconut milk and stir to combine. 3. Cover the container with storage lid and freeze for 24 hours. 4. After 24 hours, remove the lid from container and arrange into the Outer Bowl of Ninja CREAMi. 5. Install the Creamerizer Paddle onto the lid of Outer Bowl. 6. Then rotate the lid clockwise to lock. 7. Press Power button to turn on the unit. 8. Then press Smoothie Bowl button. 9. When the program is completed, turn the Outer Bowl and release it from the machine. 10. Transfer the smoothie into serving bowls and serve immediately.

Raspberry & Mango Smoothie Bowl

Prep time: 5 minutes | Cook time: 3 minutes | Serves 2

¾ cup frozen mango chunks	2 tablespoons avocado flesh
½ cup frozen raspberries	1 tablespoon agave nectar
½ cup whole milk Greek yogurt	

1. In a large bowl, add all the ingredients and mix well. 2. Transfer the mixture into an empty Ninja CREAMi pint container. 3. Cover the container with the storage lid and freeze for 24 hours. 4. After 24 hours, remove the lid from container and arrange into the outer bowl of Ninja CREAMi. 5. Install the "Creamerizer Paddle" onto the lid of outer bowl. 6. Then rotate the lid clockwise to lock. 7. Press "Power" button to turn on the unit. 8. Then press "SMOOTHIE BOWL" button. 9. When the program is completed, turn the outer bowl and release it from the machine. 10. Transfer the smoothie into serving bowls and serve immediately.

Gator Smoothies

Prep time: 5 minutes | Cook time: 5 minutes | Serves 1

1 cup ice	drink
1 cup grape-flavored sports	1 scoop vanilla ice cream

1. Add the ice, sports drink, and ice cream into an empty ninja CREAMi Pint. 2. Place the Ninja CREAMi Pint into the outer bowl. Place the outer bowl with the Pint in it into the ninja CREAMi machine and turn until the outer bowl locks into place. Push the SMOOTHIE button. During the SMOOTHIE function, the ingredients will mix together and become very creamy. 3. Once the SMOOTHIE function has ended, turn the outer bowl and release it from the ninja CREAMi machine. 4. Pour into a tall glass.

Green Monster Smoothie

Prep time: 5 minutes | Cook time: 10 minutes | Serves 1

½ cup baby spinach	¼ cup chopped carrots
½ apple, peeled, cored, and	¼ cup orange juice
chopped	¼ cup fresh strawberries
½ banana, sliced	¼ cup ice

1. Put the spinach, apples, bananas, carrots, orange juice, strawberries, and ice into an empty ninja CREAMi Pint. 2. Place the Ninja CREAMi Pint into the outer bowl. Place the outer bowl with the Pint in it into the ninja CREAMi machine and turn until the outer bowl locks into place. Push the SMOOTHIE button. During the SMOOTHIE function, the ingredients will mix together and become very creamy. 3. Once the SMOOTHIE function has ended, turn the outer bowl and release it from the ninja CREAMi machine. 4. Scoop the smoothie into a glass.

Vanilla Pumpkin Pie Smoothie

Prep time: 5 minutes | Cook time: 10 minutes | Serves 1

4 ounces pumpkin pie filling (such as Libby's)	¼ cup vanilla-flavored soy milk
½ cup vanilla frozen yogurt	½ teaspoon ground cinnamon
¼ cup ice	1 pinch ground nutmeg
	⅛ teaspoon vanilla extract

1. Combine the pumpkin pie filling, frozen yogurt, ice, soy milk, cinnamon, nutmeg, and vanilla extract and put into an empty ninja CREAMi Pint. 2. Place the Ninja CREAMi Pint into the outer bowl. Place the outer bowl with the Pint in it into the ninja CREAMi machine and turn until the outer bowl locks into place. Push the SMOOTHIE button. During the SMOOTHIE function, the ingredients will mix together and become very creamy. 3. Once the SMOOTHIE function has ended, turn the outer bowl and release it from the ninja CREAMi machine. 4. Pour the smoothie into a glass.

Fruity Coffee Smoothie Bowl

Prep time: 5 minutes | Cook time: 3 minutes | Serves 4

1 cup brewed coffee	1 cup fresh raspberries
½ cup oat milk	1 large banana, peeled and sliced
2 tablespoons almond butter	

1. In a high-speed blender add all the ingredients and pulse until smooth. 2. Transfer the mixture into an empty Ninja CREAMi pint container. 3. Cover the container with the storage lid and freeze for 24 hours. 4. After 24 hours, remove the lid from container and arrange into the outer bowl of Ninja CREAMi. 5. Install the "Creamerizer Paddle" onto the lid of outer bowl. 6. Then rotate the lid clockwise to lock. 7. Press "Power" button to turn on the unit. 8. Then press "SMOOTHIE BOWL" button. 9. When the program is completed, turn the outer bowl and release it from the machine. 10. Transfer the smoothie into serving bowls and serve immediately.

Microwave Vanilla Cake

Prep time: 5 minutes | Cook time: 5 minutes | Serves 2

½ teaspoon vanilla extract	2 tablespoons granulated sugar
3 tablespoons whole milk	¼ cup all-purpose flour
2 tablespoons unsalted butter	Chocolate Fudge Frosting, for serving (optional)
⅛ teaspoon kosher salt	
½ teaspoon baking powder	

1. Place all the ingredients except for the frosting in a clean CREAMi Pint container in the order listed. 2. Place the pint in the outer bowl of your Ninja CREAMi, install the Creamerizer Paddle in the outer bowl lid, and lock the lid assembly onto the outer bowl. Place the bowl assembly on the motor base, and twist the handle to the right to raise the platform and lock it in place. Select the

Re-Spin function. 3. Once the machine has finished processing, place the pint container in the microwave and cook on High for 2 minutes. Check the cake for doneness—a skewer or knife inserted into the cake should come out clean, and the cake should pull away from the sides of the pint container. 4. Once the container is cool enough to handle, run a butter knife around the inside of the pint. Flip the pint over, and the cake should pop right out. 5. If you want to add frosting, slice the cake widthwise into 3 layers. Place one slice on a plate and frost the top of the layer. Lay a second slice on top of the first and frost the top. Top with the final slice of cake, then frost the top and sides of the assembled cake. 6. Cut in half and serve.

Frozen Fruit Smoothie Bowl

Prep time: 5 minutes | Cook time: 3 minutes | Serves 2

1 ripe banana, peeled and cut in 1-inch pieces	2 cups frozen fruit mix
	1¼ cups vanilla yogurt

1. In a large high-speed blender, add all the ingredients and pulse until smooth. 2. Transfer the mixture into an empty Ninja CREAMi pint container. 3. Cover the container with the storage lid and freeze for 24 hours. 4. After 24 hours, remove the lid from container and arrange into the outer bowl of Ninja CREAMi. 5. Install the "Creamerizer Paddle" onto the lid of outer bowl. 6. Then rotate the lid clockwise to lock. 7. Press "Power" button to turn on the unit. 8. Then press "SMOOTHIE BOWL" button. 9. When the program is completed, turn the outer bowl and release it from the machine. 10. Transfer the smoothie into serving bowls and serve immediately.

Peach & Grapefruit Smoothie Bowl

Prep time: 5 minutes | Cook time: 3 minutes | Serves 2

1 cup frozen peach pieces	2 tablespoons honey
1 cup vanilla Greek yogurt	¼ teaspoon vanilla extract
¼ cup fresh grapefruit juice	½ teaspoon ground cinnamon

1. In a high-speed blender, add all ingredients and pulse until smooth 2. Transfer the mixture into an empty Ninja CREAMi pint container. 3. Cover the container with the storage lid and freeze for 24 hours. 4. After 24 hours, remove the lid from container and arrange into the outer bowl of Ninja CREAMi. 5. Install the "Creamerizer Paddle" onto the lid of outer bowl. 6. Then rotate the lid clockwise to lock. 7. Press "Power" button to turn on the unit. 8. Then press "SMOOTHIE BOWL" button. 9. When the program is completed, turn the outer bowl and release it from the machine. 10. Transfer the smoothie into serving bowls and serve immediately.

Kale, Avocado & Fruit Smoothie Bowl

Prep time: 5 minutes | Cook time: 3 minutes | Serves 4

1 banana, peeled and cut into 1-inch pieces	1 cup green apple, peeled, cored and cut into 1-inch pieces
½ of avocado, peeled, pitted and cut into 1-inch pieces	¼ cup unsweetened coconut milk
1 cup fresh kale leaves	2 tablespoons agave nectar

1. In a large high-speed blender, add all the ingredients and pulse until smooth. 2. Transfer the mixture into an empty Ninja CREAMi pint container. 3. Cover the container with storage lid and freeze for 24 hours. 4. After 24 hours, remove the lid from container and arrange into the Outer Bowl of Ninja CREAMi. 5. Install the Creamerizer Paddle onto the lid of Outer Bowl. 6. Then rotate the lid clockwise to lock. 7. Press Power button to turn on the unit. 8. Then press Smoothie Bowl button. 9. When the program is completed, turn the Outer Bowl and release it from the machine. 10. Transfer the smoothie into serving bowls and serve immediately.

Papaya Smoothie Bowl

Prep time: 5 minutes | Cook time: 3 minutes | Serves 2

2 cups ripe papaya, peeled and cut into 1-inch pieces	4-6 drops liquid stevia
14 ounces (397 g) whole milk	¼ teaspoon vanilla extract

1. Place the mango pieces into an empty Ninja CREAMi pint container. 2. Top with coconut milk, stevia and vanilla extract and stir to combine. 3. Cover the container with the storage lid and freeze for 24 hours. 4. After 24 hours, remove the lid from container and arrange into the outer bowl of Ninja CREAMi. 5. Install the "Creamerizer Paddle" onto the lid of outer bowl. 6. Then rotate the lid clockwise to lock. 7. Press "Power" button to turn on the unit. 8. Then press "SMOOTHIE BOWL" button. 9. When the program is completed, turn the outer bowl and release it from the machine. 10. Transfer the smoothie into serving bowls and serve immediately.

Avocado & Banana Smoothie Bowl

Prep time: 5 minutes | Cook time: 5 minutes | Serves 4

½ cup unsweetened coconut milk	¼ teaspoon vanilla extract
¼ cup fresh apple juice	1 cup ripe avocado, peeled, pitted and cut in ½-inch pieces
2 tablespoons whey protein isolate	1 cup fresh banana, peeled and cut in ½-inch pieces
4-5 tablespoons maple syrup	

1. In a large bowl, add the coconut milk, apple juice, protein isolate, maple syrup and vanilla extract and beat until well combined. 2. Place the avocado and banana into an empty Ninja CREAMi pint container and with the back of a spoon, firmly press the fruit below the MAX FILL line. 3. Top with coconut milk mixture and mix until well combined. 4. Cover the container with the storage lid and freeze for 24 hours. 5. After 24 hours, remove the lid from container and arrange into the outer bowl of Ninja CREAMi. 6. Install the "Creamerizer Paddle" onto the lid of outer bowl. 7. Then rotate the lid clockwise to lock. 8. Press "Power" button to turn on the unit. 9. Then press "SMOOTHIE BOWL" button. 10. When the program is completed, turn the outer bowl and release it from the machine. 11. Transfer the smoothie into serving bowls and serve immediately.

Kale VS Avocado Smoothie Bowl

Prep time: 5 minutes | Cook time: 3 minutes | Serves 4

1 banana, cut into 1-inch pieces	1 cup green apple pieces
½ ripe avocado, cut into 1-inch pieces	¼ cup unsweetened coconut milk
1 cup packed kale leaves	2 tablespoons agave nectar

1. Combine the banana, avocado, kale, apple, coconut milk, and agave in a blender. Blend on high for about 1 minute until smooth. 2. Pour the base into a clean CREAMi Pint. Place the storage lid on the container and freeze for 24 hours. 3. Remove the pint from the freezer and take off the lid. Place the pint in the outer bowl of your Ninja CREAMi, install the Creamerizer Paddle in the outer bowl lid, and lock the lid assembly onto the outer bowl. Place the bowl assembly on the motor base, and twist the handle to the right to raise the platform and lock it in place. Select the Smoothie Bowl function. 4. Once the machine has finished processing, remove the smoothie bowl from the pint. Serve immediately with your desired toppings.

Orange & Mango Smoothie Bowl

Prep time: 5 minutes | Cook time: 3 minutes | Serves 2

1 cup frozen mango chunks	½ teaspoon ground turmeric
1 cup plain whole milk yogurt	⅛ teaspoon ground cinnamon
¼ cup fresh orange juice	⅛ teaspoon ground ginger
2 tablespoons maple syrup	Pinch of ground black pepper

1. In a high-speed blender, add all ingredients and pulse until smooth 2. Transfer the mixture into an empty Ninja CREAMi pint container. 3. Cover the container with the storage lid and freeze for 24 hours. 4. After 24 hours, remove the lid from container and arrange into the outer bowl of Ninja CREAMi. 5. Install the "Creamerizer Paddle" onto the lid of outer bowl. 6. Then rotate the lid clockwise to lock. 7. Press "Power" button to turn on the unit. 8. Then press "SMOOTHIE BOWL" button. 9. When the program is completed, turn the outer bowl and release it from the machine. 10. Transfer the smoothie into serving bowls and serve immediately.

Raspberry Smoothie Bowl

Prep time: 5 minutes | Cook time: 3 minutes | Serves 4

1 cup brewed coffee

½ cup oat milk

2 tablespoons almond butter

1 cup fresh raspberries

1 large banana, peeled and sliced

1. In a high-speed blender add all the ingredients and pulse until smooth. 2. Transfer the mixture into an empty Ninja CREAMi pint container. 3. Cover the container with storage lid and freeze for 24 hours. 4. After 24 hours, remove the lid from container and arrange into the Outer Bowl of Ninja CREAMi. 5. Install the Creamerizer Paddle onto the lid of Outer Bowl. 6. Then rotate the lid clockwise to lock. 7. Press Power button to turn on the unit. 8. Then press Smoothie Bowl button. 9. When the program is completed, turn the Outer Bowl and release it from the machine. 10. Transfer the smoothie into serving bowls and serve immediately.

Simple Smoothie Bowl

Prep time: 5 minutes | Cook time: 5 minutes | Serves 2

1 bottle fruit smoothie beverage

1. Pour the smoothie beverage into a clean CREAMi Pint. Place the storage lid on the container and freeze for 24 hours 2. Remove the pint from the freezer and take off the lid. Place the pint in the outer bowl of your Ninja CREAMi, install the Creamerizer Paddle in the outer bowl lid, and lock the lid assembly onto the outer bowl. Place the bowl assembly on the motor base, and twist the handle to the right to raise the platform and lock it in place. Select the Smoothie Bowl function. 3. Once the machine has finished processing, remove the smoothie bowl from the pint. Serve immediately with desired toppings.

Peaches And Cream Smoothie Bowl

Prep time: 5 minutes | Cook time: 3 minutes | Serves 4

1 can peaches in their juice

¼ cup vanilla yogurt

2 tablespoons agave nectar

1. Place the peaches in their juice, yogurt, and agave in a clean CREAMi Pint and stir to combine. Place the storage lid on the container and freeze for 24 hours. 2. Remove the pint from the freezer and take off the lid. Place the pint in the outer bowl of your Ninja CREAMi, install the Creamerizer Paddle in the outer bowl lid, and lock the lid assembly onto the outer bowl. Place the bowl assembly on the motor base, and twist the handle to the right to raise the platform and lock it in place. Select the Smoothie Bowl function. 3. Once the machine has finished processing, remove the smoothie bowl from the pint. Serve immediately with desired toppings.

Buttery Coffee Smoothie

Prep time: 5 minutes | Cook time: 5 minutes | Serves 1

1 cup brewed coffee

2 large pasteurized egg yolks

¼ cup avocado

¼ cup ice cubes

1 tablespoon coconut sugar

2 tablespoons coconut oil, melted

1. Combine the coffee, egg yolks, avocado, ice cubes, and coconut sugar in an empty ninja CREAMi Pint. 2. Place the Ninja CREAMi Pint into the outer bowl. Place the outer bowl with the Pint in it into the ninja CREAMi machine and turn until the outer bowl locks into place. Push the SMOOTHIE button. During the SMOOTHIE function, the ingredients will mix together and become very creamy. 3. Once the SMOOTHIE function has ended, turn the outer bowl and release it from the ninja CREAMi machine. 4. Scoop the smoothie into a tall glass.

Avocado Smoothie

Prep time: 5 minutes | Cook time: 5 minutes | Serves 1

½ ripe avocado, peeled, halved, and pitted

½ cup milk

¼ cup vanilla yogurt

1½ tablespoons honey

4 ice cubes

1. Combine the avocado, milk, yogurt, honey, and ice cubes in an empty ninja CREAMi Pint. 2. Place the Ninja CREAMi Pint into the outer bowl. Place the outer bowl with the Pint in it into the ninja CREAMi machine and turn until the outer bowl locks into place. Push the SMOOTHIE button. During the SMOOTHIE function, the ingredients will mix together and become very creamy. 3. Once the SMOOTHIE function has ended, turn the outer bowl and release it from the ninja CREAMi machine. 4. Pour the smoothie into glasses.

Blueberry Smoothie Bowl

Prep time: 5 minutes | Cook time: 10 minutes | Serves 1

¾ cups Ocean Spray blueberry juice cocktail, chilled

⅔ cup fresh blueberries, cleaned

and rinsed

½ cup vanilla yogurt or vanilla frozen yogurt

1. Puree the blueberries. 2. Put the pureed blueberries, blueberry juice cocktail, and yogurt into an empty ninja CREAMi Pint 3. Place the Ninja CREAMi Pint into the outer bowl. Place the outer bowl with the Pint in it into the ninja CREAMi machine and turn until the outer bowl locks into place. Push the smoothie button. During the smoothie function, the ingredients will mix together and become very creamy. 4. Once the smoothie function has ended, turn the outer bowl and release it from the ninja CREAMi machine. 5. Scoop smoothie into a bowl.

Chocolate Fudge Frosting

Prep time: 5 minutes | Cook time: 5 minutes | Serves 1

½ cup cold unsalted butter, cut in 8 pieces	cocoa powder
1½ cups confectioners' sugar	1 tablespoon heavy (whipping) cream
2 tablespoons dark unsweetened	1 teaspoon vanilla extract

1. Place all the ingredients in a clean CREAMi Pint in the order listed. 2. Place the pint in the outer bowl of your Ninja CREAMi, install the Creamerizer Paddle in the outer bowl lid, and lock the lid assembly onto the outer bowl. Place the bowl assembly on the motor base, and twist the handle to the right to raise the platform and lock it in place. Select the Re-Spin function. 3. Once the machine has finished processing, the frosting should be smooth and easily scoopable with a spoon. If the frosting is too thick, select the Re-Spin function again and process until creamy and smooth.

Vodka Smoothie

Prep time: 5 minutes | Cook time: 5 minutes | Serves 2

3 fluid ounces vodka	2 scoops orange sherbet
9 fluid ounces orange juice	½ cup crushed ice
½ cup frozen strawberries	

1. Mix the vodka, orange juice, strawberries, orange sherbet, and ice in an empty ninja CREAMi Pint. 2. Place the Ninja CREAMi Pint into the outer bowl. Place the outer bowl with the Pint in it into the ninja CREAMi machine and turn until the outer bowl locks into place. Push the SMOOTHIE button. During the SMOOTHIE function, the ingredients will mix together and become very creamy. 3. Once the SMOOTHIE function has ended, turn the outer bowl and release it from the ninja CREAMi machine. 4. Scoop the smoothie into glass cups.

Green Fruity Smoothie Bowl

Prep time: 5 minutes | Cook time: 5 minutes | Serves 2

1 banana, peeled and cut into 1-inch pieces	1 cup green apple, peeled, cored and cut into 1-inch pieces
½ of avocado, peeled, pitted and cut into 1-inch pieces	¼ cup unsweetened coconut milk
1 cup fresh kale leaves	2 tablespoons agave nectar

1. In a large high-speed blender, add all the ingredients and pulse until smooth. 2. Transfer the mixture into an empty Ninja CREAMi pint container. 3. Cover the container with the storage lid and freeze for 24 hours. 4. After 24 hours, remove the lid from container and arrange into the outer bowl of Ninja CREAMi. 5. Install the "Creamerizer Paddle" onto the lid of outer bowl. 6. Then rotate the lid clockwise to lock. 7. Press "Power" button to turn on the unit. 8. Then press "SMOOTHIE BOWL" button. 9. When the program is completed, turn the outer bowl and release it from the machine. 10. Transfer the smoothie into serving bowls and serve immediately.

Oat Banana Smoothie Bowl

Prep time: 5 minutes | Cook time: 1 minutes | Serves 2

½ cup water	½ cup banana, peeled and sliced
¼ cup quick oats	3 tablespoons honey
1 cup vanilla Greek yogurt	

1. In a small microwave-safe bowl, add the water and oats and microwave on High or about one minute. 2. Remove from the microwave and stir in the yogurt, banana and honey until well combined. 3. Transfer the mixture into an empty Ninja CREAMi pint container. 4. Cover the container with storage lid and freeze for 24 hours. 5. After 24 hours, remove the lid from container and arrange into the Outer Bowl of Ninja CREAMi. 6. Install the Creamerizer Paddle onto the lid of Outer Bowl. 7. Then rotate the lid clockwise to lock. 8. Press Power button to turn on the unit. 9. Then press Smoothie Bowl button. 10. When the program is completed, turn the Outer Bowl and release it from the machine. 11. Transfer the smoothie into serving bowls and serve with your favorite topping.

Mango & Orange Smoothie Bowl

Prep time: 5 minutes | Cook time: 3 minutes | Serves 2

1 cup frozen mango chunks	½ teaspoon ground turmeric
1 cup plain whole milk yogurt	⅛ teaspoon ground cinnamon
¼ cup fresh orange juice	⅛ teaspoon ground ginger
2 tablespoons maple syrup	Pinch of ground black pepper

1. In a high-speed blender, add all ingredients and pulse until smooth 2. Transfer the mixture into an empty Ninja CREAMi pint container. 3. Cover the container with storage lid and freeze for 24 hours. 4. After 24 hours, remove the lid from container and arrange into the Outer Bowl of Ninja CREAMi. 5. Install the Creamerizer Paddle onto the lid of Outer Bowl. 6. Then rotate the lid clockwise to lock. 7. Press Power button to turn on the unit. 8. Then press Smoothie Bowl button. 9. When the program is completed, turn the Outer Bowl and release it from the machine. 10. Transfer the smoothie into serving bowls and serve immediately.

Pineapple Smoothie Bowl

Prep time: 5 minutes | Cook time: 5 minutes | Serves 4

2 ripe bananas, peeled and cut in 1-inch pieces	¼ cup yogurt
1 cup fresh pineapple, chopped	2 tablespoons honey

1. In a large bowl, add all the ingredients and beat until well combined. 2. Transfer the mixture into an empty Ninja CREAMi pint container. 3. Cover the container with storage lid and freeze for 24 hours. 4. After 24 hours, remove the lid from container and arrange into the Outer Bowl of Ninja CREAMi. 5. Install the Creamerizer Paddle onto the lid of Outer Bowl. 6. Then rotate the lid clockwise to lock. 7. Press Power button to turn on the unit. 8. Then press Smoothie Bowl button. 9. When the program is completed, turn the Outer Bowl and release it from the machine. 10. Transfer the smoothie into serving bowls and serve immediately.

Piña Smoothie Bowl

Prep time: 5 minutes | Cook time: 5 minutes | Serves 4

1½ cups canned pineapple chunks in their juice	½ cup canned coconut milk
	1 tablespoon agave nectar

1. Pour the pineapple chunks in their juice, coconut milk, and agave into a clean CREAMi Pint and stir to combine. Place the storage lid on the container and freeze for 24 hours. 2. Remove the pint from the freezer and take off the lid. Place the pint in the outer bowl of your Ninja CREAMi, install the Creamerizer Paddle in the outer bowl lid, and lock the lid assembly onto the outer bowl. Place the bowl assembly on the motor base, and twist the handle to the right to raise the platform and lock it in place. Select the Smoothie Bowl function. 3. Once the machine has finished processing, remove the smoothie bowl from the pint. Serve immediately with your desired toppings.

Piescream

Prep time: 5 minutes | Cook time: 5 minutes | Serves 4

1 can cherry pie filling	cracker crust
1 store-bought frozen graham	1 container whipped topping

1. Fill a clean CREAMi Pint to the max fill line with the pie filing. Place the storage lid on the container and freeze for 24 hours. 2. Remove the pint from the freezer and take off the lid. Place the pint in the outer bowl of your Ninja CREAMi, install the Creamerizer Paddle in the outer bowl lid, and lock the lid assembly onto the outer bowl. Place the bowl assembly on the motor base, and twist the handle to the right to raise the platform and lock it in place.

Select the Sorbet function. 3. Once the machine has finished processing, remove the sorbet from the pint. Let it thaw until it is spreadable, about 5 minutes. 4. Spread the pie filling sorbet onto the frozen graham cracker crust. Spread the whipped topping on top of the filling. Freeze for 4 to 6 hours or until hardened. When ready to serve, remove from the freezer. Let the pie thaw just until you can slice it with a knife.

Mixed Berries Smoothie Bowl

Prep time: 5 minutes | Cook time: 5 minutes | Serves 4

¾ cup fresh strawberries, hulled and quartered	¾ cup fresh blackberries
¾ cup fresh raspberries	¼ cup plain Greek yogurt
¾ cup fresh blueberries	1 tablespoon honey

1. In an empty Ninja CREAMi pint container, place the berries and with the back of a spoon, firmly press the berries below the Max Fill line. 2. Add the yogurt and honey and stir to combine. 3. Cover the container with storage lid and freeze for 24 hours. 4. After 24 hours, remove the lid from container and arrange into the Outer Bowl of Ninja CREAMi. 5. Install the Creamerizer Paddle onto the lid of Outer Bowl. 6. Then rotate the lid clockwise to lock. 7. Press Power button to turn on the unit. 8. Then press Smoothie Bowl button. 9. When the program is completed, turn the Outer Bowl and release it from the machine. 10. Transfer the smoothie into serving bowls and serve immediately.

Fruity Coconut Smoothie Bowl

Prep time: 5 minutes | Cook time: 5 minutes | Serves 2

½ of ripe banana, peeled and cut in ½-inch pieces	½ cup unsweetened canned coconut milk
¼ cup coconut rum	¾ cup pineapple juice
¼ cup unsweetened coconut cream	2 tablespoons fresh lime juice

1. In a large bowl, add all the ingredients and beat until well combined. 2. Transfer the mixture into an empty Ninja CREAMi pint container. 3. Cover the container with the storage lid and freeze for 24 hours. 4. After 24 hours, remove the lid from container and arrange into the outer bowl of Ninja CREAMi. 5. Install the "Creamerizer Paddle" onto the lid of outer bowl. 6. Then rotate the lid clockwise to lock. 7. Press "Power" button to turn on the unit. 8. Then press "SMOOTHIE BOWL" button. 9. When the program is completed, turn the outer bowl and release it from the machine. 10. Transfer the smoothie into serving bowl sand serve immediately.

Energy Elixir Smoothie

Prep time: 5 minutes | Cook time: 5 minutes | Serves 1

½ cup spring salad greens

½ cup frozen red grapes

½ chopped frozen banana

½ cored and chopped frozen

pear

2 tablespoons walnuts

Water as needed

1. Layer the salad greens, red grapes, banana, pear, walnuts, and enough water to cover the mixture in an empty ninja CREAMi Pint. 2. Place the Ninja CREAMi Pint into the outer bowl. Place the outer bowl with the Pint in it into the ninja CREAMi machine and turn until the outer bowl locks into place. Push the SMOOTHIE button. During the SMOOTHIE function, the ingredients will mix together and become very creamy. 3. Once the SMOOTHIE function has ended, turn the outer bowl and release it from the ninja CREAMi machine. 4. Scoop the smoothie into a glass.

Pumpkin & Banana Smoothie Bowl

Prep time: 5 minutes | Cook time: 3 minutes | Serves 2

1 cup canned pumpkin puree

⅓ cup plain Greek yogurt

1½ tablespoons maple syrup

1 teaspoon vanilla extract

1 teaspoon pumpkin pie spice

1 frozen banana, peeled and cut in ½-inch pieces

1. In an empty Ninja CREAMi pint container, add the pumpkin puree, yogurt, maple syrup, vanilla extract, and pumpkin pie spice and mix well. 2. Add the banana pieces and stir to combine. 3. Transfer the mixture into an empty Ninja CREAMi pint container. 4. Arrange the container into the outer bowl of Ninja CREAMi. 5. Install the "Creamerizer Paddle" onto the lid of outer bowl. 6. Then rotate the lid clockwise to lock. 7. Press "Power" button to turn on the unit. 8. Then press "SMOOTHIE BOWL" button. 9. When the program is completed, turn the outer bowl and release it from the machine. 10. Transfer the smoothie into serving bowls and serve immediately.

Chocolate, Peanut Butter & Banana Smoothie

Prep time: 5 minutes | Cook time: 5 minutes | Serves 2

1 cup chocolate pudding

1 tablespoon creamy peanut butter

1 large ripe banana, cut into pieces

⅔ cup reduced-fat milk

½ cup ice cubes

Reddi-wip chocolate dairy whipped topping

1. Mash the bananas in a large bowl and add all the other ingredients except for the whipped topping. Combine and put into the ninja CREAMi Pint. 2. Place the Pint into the outer bowl. Place the outer bowl with the Pint in it into the ninja CREAMi machine and turn until the outer bowl locks into place. Push the SMOOTHIE button. The ingredients will mix together and become very creamy. 3. Once the SMOOTHIE function has ended, turn the outer bowl and release it from the ninja CREAMi machine. 4. Scoop the smoothie into glass bowls to serve.

Raspberry & Orange Smoothie Bowl

Prep time: 5 minutes | Cook time: 5 minutes | Serves 2

2 cups fresh raspberries

½ cup vanilla yogurt

¼ cup fresh orange juice

1 tablespoon honey

1. In an empty Ninja CREAMi pint container, place the raspberries and with the back of a spoon, firmly press the berries below the MAX FILL line. 2. Add the yogurt, orange juice and honey and stir to combine. 3. Cover the container with the storage lid and freeze for 24 hours. 4. After 24 hours, remove the lid from container and arrange into the outer bowl of Ninja CREAMi. 5. Install the "Creamerizer Paddle" onto the lid of outer bowl. 6. Then rotate the lid clockwise to lock. 7. Press "Power" button to turn on the unit. 8. Then press "SMOOTHIE BOWL" button. 9. When the program is completed, turn the outer bowl and release it from the machine. 10. Transfer the smoothie into serving bowls and serve immediately.

Chapter 5 Sorbet Recipes

Chapter 5 Sorbet Recipes

Blueberry Lemon Sorbet

Prep time: 5 minutes | Cook time: 5 minutes | Serves 1

1 tablespoon cream cheese	⅓ cup blueberries (fresh or
¼ cup milk	frozen)
1½ cups lemonade	

1. In a medium mixing bowl, whisk together the softened cream cheese and the milk. Make an effort to integrate the two as much as possible. Some little bits of cream cheese may remain, but that's fine as long as they're small. 2. Add the lemonade and stir thoroughly. 3. Pour the mixture into a ninja CREAMi Pint container, add the blueberries and freeze on a level surface in a cold freezer for a full 24 hours. 4. After 24 hours, remove the Pint from the freezer. Remove the lid. 5. Place the Ninja CREAMi Pint into the outer bowl. Place the outer bowl with the Pint in it into the ninja CREAMi machine and turn until the outer bowl locks into place. Push the SORBET button. During the SORBET function, the sorbet will mix together and become very creamy. This should take approximately 2 minutes. 6. Once the SORBET function has ended, turn the outer bowl and release it from the ninja CREAMi machine. 7. Your sorbet is ready to eat! Enjoy! 8. Place the outer bowl with the Pint back into the ninja CREAMi machine and lock it into place if the sorbet isn't quite creamy enough. Select the RE-SPIN option. Remove the outer bowl from the Ninja CREAMi after the RE-SPIN cycle is complete.

Grape Sorbet

Prep time: 5 minutes | Cook time: 5 minutes | Serves 4

¾ cup frozen grape juice concentrate	1½ cups water
	1 tablespoon fresh lemon juice

1. In a bowl, add all the ingredients and beat until well combined. 2. Transfer the mixture into an empty Ninja CREAMi pint container. 3. Cover the container with storage lid and freeze for 24 hours. 4. After 24 hours, remove the lid from container and arrange into the Outer Bowl of Ninja CREAMi. 5. Install the Creamerizer Paddle onto the lid of Outer Bowl. 6. Then rotate the lid clockwise to lock. 7. Press Power button to turn on the unit. 8. Then press Sorbet button. 9. When the program is completed, turn the Outer Bowl and release it from the machine. 10. Transfer the sorbet into serving bowls and serve immediately.

Coconut Lime Sorbet

Prep time: 5 minutes | Cook time: 30 minutes | Serves 5

1 can coconut cream	½ tablespoon lime zest
½ cup coconut water	¼ teaspoon coconut extract
¼ cup lime juice	(optional)

1. Combine the coconut cream, coconut water, lime juice, lime zest, and coconut extract in a mixing bowl. Cover with plastic wrap and refrigerate for at least 1 hour, or until the flavors have melded. 2. Add the mixture to the Ninja CREAMi Pint container and freeze on a level surface in a cold freezer for a full 24 hours. 3. After 24 hours, remove the Pint from the freezer. Remove the lid. 4. Place the Ninja CREAMi Pint into the outer bowl. Place the outer bowl with the Pint in it into the ninja CREAMi machine and turn until the outer bowl locks into place. Push the SORBET button. During the SORBET function, the sorbet will mix together and become very creamy. This should take approximately 2 minutes. 5. Once the SORBET function has ended, turn the outer bowl and release it from the ninja CREAMi machine. 6. Your sorbet is ready to eat! Enjoy!

Cherry-berry Rosé Sorbet

Prep time: 5 minutes | Cook time: 10 minutes | Serves 3

2 cups frozen cherry-berry fruit blend	¼ cup white sugar, or to taste
½ cup rosé wine, or as needed	¼ medium lemon, juiced

1. Add all ingredients to a bowl and mix until the sugar dissolves. Place the mixture in the ninja CREAMi Pint container and freeze on a level surface in a cold freezer for a full 24 hours. 2. After 24 hours, remove the Pint from the freezer. Remove the lid. 3. Place the Ninja CREAMi Pint into the outer bowl. Place the outer bowl with the Pint in it into the ninja CREAMi machine and turn until the outer bowl locks into place. Push the SORBET button. During the SORBET function, the sorbet will mix together and become very creamy. This should take approximately 2 minutes. 4. Once the SORBET function has ended, turn the outer bowl and release it from the ninja CREAMi machine. 5. Your sorbet is ready to eat! Enjoy!

Blueberry & Pomegranate Sorbet

Prep time: 5 minutes | Cook time: 5 minutes | Serves 4

1 can blueberries in light syrup	½ cup pomegranate juice

1. In an empty Ninja CREAMi pint container, place the blueberries and top with syrup. 2. Add in the pomegranate juice and stir to combine. 3. Cover the container with the storage lid and freeze for 24 hours. 4. After 24 hours, remove the lid from container and arrange into the outer bowl of Ninja CREAMi. 5. Install the "Creamerizer Paddle" onto the lid of outer bowl. 6. Then rotate the lid clockwise to lock 7. Press "Power" button to turn on the unit. 8. Then press "SORBET" button. 9. When the program is completed, turn the outer bowl and release it from the machine. 10. Transfer the sorbet into serving bowls and serve immediately.

Lime Beer Sorbet

Prep time: 5 minutes | Cook time: 5 minutes | Serves 4

¾ cup beer	½ cup fresh lime juice
⅔ cup water	¼ cup granulated sugar

1. In a high-speed blender, add all the ingredients and pulse until smooth. 2. Set aside for about 5 minutes. 3. Transfer the mixture into an empty Ninja CREAMi pint container. 4. Cover the container with the storage lid and freeze for 24 hours. 5. After 24 hours, remove the lid from container and arrange into the outer bowl of Ninja CREAMi. 6. Install the "Creamerizer Paddle" onto the lid of outer bowl. 7. Then rotate the lid clockwise to lock. 8. Press "Power" button to turn on the unit. 9. Then press "SORBET" button. 10. When the program is completed, turn the outer bowl and release it from the machine 11. Transfer the sorbet into serving bowls and serve immediately.

Avocado Lime Sorbet

Prep time: 5 minutes | Cook time: 5 minutes | Serves 4

¾ cup water	1 large ripe avocado, peeled,
2 tablespoons light corn syrup	pitted and chopped
Pinch of sea salt	3 ounces fresh lime juice
⅔ cup granulated sugar	

1. In a medium saucepan, add water, corn syrup and salt and beat until well combined. 2. Place the saucepan over medium heat. 3. Slowly add the sugar, continuously beating until well combined and bring to a boil. 4. Remove the saucepan from heat and set aside to cool completely. 5. In a high-speed blender, add the sugar mixture, avocado and lime juice and pulse until smooth. 6. Transfer the mixture into an empty Ninja CREAMi pint container. 7. Cover the container with the storage lid and freeze for 24 hours. 8. After 24 hours, remove the lid from container and arrange into the outer

bowl of Ninja CREAMi. 9. Install the "Creamerizer Paddle" onto the lid of outer bowl. 10. Then rotate the lid clockwise to lock. 11. Press "Power" button to turn on the unit. 12. Then press "SORBET" button. 13. When the program is completed, turn the outer bowl and release it from the machine. 14. Transfer the sorbet into serving bowls and serve immediately.

Lemony Herb Sorbet

Prep time: 5 minutes | Cook time: 6 minutes | Serves 4

½ cup water	2 large fresh basil sprigs,
¼ cup granulated sugar	stemmed
2 large fresh dill sprigs,	1 cup ice water
stemmed	2 tablespoons fresh lemon juice

1. In a small saucepan, add sugar and water and over medium heat and cook for about five minutes or until the sugar is dissolved, stirring continuously. 2. Stir in the herb sprigs and remove from the heat. 3. Add the ice water and lemon juice and stir to combine. 4. Transfer the mixture into an empty Ninja CREAMi pint container. 5. Cover the container with storage lid and freeze for 24 hours. 6. After 24 hours, remove the lid from container and arrange into the Outer Bowl of Ninja CREAMi. 7. Install the Creamerizer Paddle onto the lid of Outer Bowl. 8. Then rotate the lid clockwise to lock. 9. Press Power button to turn on the unit. 10. Then press Sorbet button. 11. When the program is completed, turn the Outer Bowl and release it from the machine. 12. Transfer the sorbet into serving bowls and serve immediately.

Mango Sorbet

Prep time: 5 minutes | Cook time: 5 minutes | Serves 4

4 cups mangoes, peeled, pitted	⅓-½ cup sugar
and chopped	¼ cup fresh lime juice
½ cup water	2 tablespoons Chamoy

1. In a high-speed blender, add mangoes and water and pulse until smooth. 2. Through a fine-mesh strainer, strain the mango puree into a large bowl. 3. Add the sugar, lime juice and chamoy and stir to combine. 4. Transfer the mixture into an empty Ninja CREAMi pint container. 5. Cover the container with storage lid and freeze for 24 hours. 6. After 24 hours, remove the lid from container and arrange into the Outer Bowl of Ninja CREAMi. 7. Install the Creamerizer Paddle onto the lid of Outer Bowl. 8. Then rotate the lid clockwise to lock. 9. Press Power button to turn on the unit. 10. Then press Sorbet button. 11. When the program is completed, turn the Outer Bowl and release it from the machine. 12. Transfer the sorbet into serving bowls and serve immediately.

Raspberry Lime Sorbet

Prep time: 5 minutes | Cook time: 5 minutes | Serves 4

2 cups fresh raspberries

5 ounces simple syrup

6 tablespoons fresh lime juice

1. In an empty Ninja CREAMi pint container, add all the ingredients and mix well. 2. Cover the container with the storage lid and freeze for 24 hours. 3. After 24 hours, remove the lid from container and arrange into the outer bowl of Ninja CREAMi. 4. Install the "Creamerizer Paddle" onto the lid of outer bowl. 5. Then rotate the lid clockwise to lock. 6. Press "Power" button to turn on the unit. 7. Then press "SORBET" button. 8. When the program is completed, turn the outer bowl and release it from the machine. 9. Transfer the sorbet into serving bowls and serve immediately.

Banana Sorbet

Prep time: 5 minutes | Cook time: 5 minutes | Serves 2

1 frozen banana

1 teaspoon cold water

2 teaspoons caramel sauce

1. Add the banana, water, and caramel sauce into the ninja CREAMi Pint container and freeze on a level surface in a cold freezer for a full 24 hours. 2. After 24 hours, remove the Pint from the freezer. Remove the lid. 3. Place the Ninja CREAMi Pint into the outer bowl. Place the outer bowl with the Pint in it into the ninja CREAMi machine and turn until the outer bowl locks into place. Push the SORBET button. During the SORBET function, the sorbet will mix together and become very creamy. This should take approximately 2 minutes. 4. Once the SORBET function has ended, turn the outer bowl and release it from the ninja CREAMi machine.

Raspberry Sorbet

Prep time: 5 minutes | Cook time: 5 minutes | Serves 4

3 cups fresh raspberries

⅓ cup water

⅓ cup sugar

¾ cup berry punch

1. In a high-speed blender, add all the ingredients and pulse until smooth. 2. Transfer the mixture into an empty Ninja CREAMi pint container. 3. Cover the container with storage lid and freeze for 24 hours. 4. After 24 hours, remove the lid from container and arrange into the Outer Bowl of Ninja CREAMi. 5. Install the Creamerizer Paddle onto the lid of Outer Bowl. 6. Then rotate the lid clockwise to lock. 7. Press Power button to turn on the unit. 8. Then press Sorbet button. 9. When the program is completed, turn the Outer Bowl and release it from the machine. 10. Transfer the sorbet into serving bowls and serve immediately.

Plum Sorbet

Prep time: 5 minutes | Cook time: 5 minutes | Serves 4

1 can plums

1. Place the plums into an empty Ninja CREAMi pint container. 2. Cover the container with storage lid and freeze for 24 hours. 3. After 24 hours, remove the lid from container and arrange into the Outer Bowl of Ninja CREAMi. 4. Install the Creamerizer Paddle onto the lid of Outer Bowl. 5. Then rotate the lid clockwise to lock. 6. Press Power button to turn on the unit. 7. Then press Sorbet button. 8. When the program is completed, turn the Outer Bowl and release it from the machine. 9. Transfer the sorbet into serving bowls and serve immediately.

Pineapple & Rum Sorbet

Prep time: 5 minutes | Cook time: 5 minutes | Serves 4

¾ cup piña colada mix

¼ cup rum

2 tablespoons granulated sugar

1½ cups frozen pineapple chunks

1. In a high-speed blender, add all the ingredients and pulse until smooth. 2. Transfer the mixture into an empty Ninja CREAMi pint container. 3. Cover the container with storage lid and freeze for 24 hours. 4. After 24 hours, remove the lid from container and arrange into the Outer Bowl of Ninja CREAMi. 5. Install the Creamerizer Paddle onto the lid of Outer Bowl. 6. Then rotate the lid clockwise to lock. 7. Press Power button to turn on the unit. 8. Then press Sorbet button. 9. When the program is completed, turn the Outer Bowl and release it from the machine. 10. Transfer the sorbet into serving bowls and serve immediately.

Peach Sorbet

Prep time: 5 minutes | Cook time: 5 minutes | Serves 4

1 cup passionfruit seltzer

3 tablespoons agave nectar

1 can peaches in heavy syrup, drained

1. In a bowl, add the seltzer and agave and beat until agave is dissolved. 2. Place the peaches into an empty Ninja CREAMi pint container and top with seltzer mixture. 3. Cover the container with storage lid and freeze for 24 hours. 4. After 24 hours, remove the lid from container and arrange into the Outer Bowl of Ninja CREAMi. 5. Install the Creamerizer Paddle onto the lid of Outer Bowl. 6. Then rotate the lid clockwise to lock. 7. Press Power button to turn on the unit. 8. Then press Sorbet button. 9. When the program is completed, turn the Outer Bowl and release it from the machine. 10. Transfer the sorbet into serving bowls and serve immediately.

Italian Ice Sorbet

Prep time: 5 minutes | Cook time: 5 minutes | Serves 1

12 ounces lemonade	is quite tart, use 6 ounces of
Sugar or your preferred	lemonade and 6 ounces of
sweetener to taste (optional)	water instead of 12 ounces of
If the lemonade you're using	lemonade

1. Pour the lemonade (or lemonade and water mixture) into a ninja CREAMi Pint container and freeze on a level surface in a cold freezer for a full 24 hours. 2. After 24 hours, remove the Pint from the freezer. Remove the lid. 3. Place the Ninja CREAMi Pint into the outer bowl. Place the outer bowl with the Pint in it into the ninja CREAMi machine and turn until the outer bowl locks into place. Push the SORBET button. During the SORBET function, the sorbet will mix together and become very creamy. This should take approximately 2 minutes. 4. Once the SORBET function has ended, turn the outer bowl and release it from the ninja CREAMi machine.

Pear Sorbet

Prep time: 5 minutes | Cook time: 5 minutes | Serves 4

1 can pears in light syrup

1. Place the pear pieces into an empty Ninja CREAMi to the MAX FILL line. 2. Cover the orange pieces with syrup from the can. 3. Cover the container with the storage lid and freeze for 24 hours. 4. After 24 hours, remove the lid from container and arrange into the outer bowl of Ninja CREAMi. 5. Install the "Creamerizer Paddle" onto the lid of outer bowl. 6. Then rotate the lid clockwise to lock. 7. Press "Power" button to turn on the unit. 8. Then press "SORBET" button. 9. When the program is completed, turn the outer bowl and release it from the machine. 10. Transfer the sorbet into serving bowls and serve immediately.

Celery Sorbet

Prep time: 5 minutes | Cook time: 5 minutes | Serves 3

½ cup white sugar	Pinch of salt, or to taste
½ cup cold water	½ medium lime, juiced
½ pound trimmed celery	

1. In a saucepan over medium heat, combine the sugar and water until it just begins to boil. Remove the pan from the heat. While the other ingredients are being prepared, cool the simple syrup to room temperature. 2. The celery should be cut into tiny pieces. Combine the salt, lime juice, and the cooled simple syrup in a mixing bowl. Blend until completely smooth. 3. Fill a sieve with the mixture. Using a spoon, press the mixture through the strainer until all of the juice has been removed. Cover and refrigerate the juice for at least 1 hour or until completely cooled. 4. Put the cooled mixture into

the ninja CREAMi Pint container and freeze on a level surface in a cold freezer for a full 24 hours. 5. After 24 hours, remove the Pint from the freezer. Remove the lid. 6. Place the Ninja CREAMi Pint into the outer bowl. Place the outer bowl with the Pint in it into the ninja CREAMi machine and turn until the outer bowl locks into place. Push the SORBET button. During the SORBET function, the sorbet will mix together and become very creamy. This should take approximately 2 minutes. 7. Once the SORBET function has ended, turn the outer bowl and release it from the ninja CREAMi machine. 8. Your sorbet is ready to eat! Enjoy!

Acai & Fruit Sorbet

Prep time: 5 minutes | Cook time: 5 minutes | Serves 4

1 packet frozen acai	¼ cup granulated sugar
½ cup blackberries	1 cup water
½ cup banana, peeled and sliced	

1. In a high-speed blender, add all the ingredients and pulse until smooth. 2. Transfer the mixture into an empty Ninja CREAMi pint container. 3. Cover the container with storage lid and freeze for 24 hours. 4. After 24 hours, remove the lid from container and arrange into the Outer Bowl of Ninja CREAMi. 5. Install the Creamerizer Paddle onto the lid of Outer Bowl. 6. Then rotate the lid clockwise to lock. 7. Press Power button to turn on the unit. 8. Then press Sorbet button. 9. When the program is completed, turn the Outer Bowl and release it from the machine. 10. Transfer the sorbet into serving bowls and serve immediately.

Mango Chamoy Sorbet

Prep time: 5 minutes | Cook time: 5 minutes | Serves 4

4 cups mangoes, peeled, pitted and chopped	⅓-½ cup sugar
½ cup water	¼ cup fresh lime juice
	2 tablespoons chamoy

1. In a high-speed blender, add mangoes and water and pulse until smooth. 2. Through a fine-mesh strainer, strain the mango puree into a large bowl. 3. Add the sugar, lime juice and chamoy and stir to combine. 4. Transfer the mixture into an empty Ninja CREAMi pint container. 5. Cover the container with the storage lid and freeze for 24 hours. 6. After 24 hours, remove the lid from container and arrange into the outer bowl of Ninja CREAMi. 7. Install the "Creamerizer Paddle" onto the lid of outer bowl. 8. Then rotate the lid clockwise to lock. 9. Press "Power" button to turn on the unit. 10. Then press "SORBET" button. 11. When the program is completed, turn the outer bowl and release it from the machine. 12. Transfer the sorbet into serving bowls and serve immediately.

Cherry Sorbet

Prep time: 5 minutes | Cook time: 5 minutes | Serves 4

1½ cups cola

⅓ cup maraschino cherries

⅓ cup spiced rum

¼ cup water

1 tablespoon fresh lime juice

1. In a high-speed blender, add all the ingredients and pulse until smooth. 2. Transfer the mixture into an empty Ninja CREAMi pint container. 3. Cover the container with the storage lid and freeze for 24 hours. 4. After 24 hours, remove the lid from container and arrange into the outer bowl of Ninja CREAMi. 5. Install the "Creamerizer Paddle" onto the lid of outer bowl. 6. Then rotate the lid clockwise to lock. 7. Press "Power" button to turn on the unit. 8. Then press "SORBET" button. 9. When the program is completed, turn the outer bowl and release it from the machine. 10. Transfer the sorbet into serving bowls and serve immediately.

Kiwi & Strawberry Sorbet

Prep time: 5 minutes | Cook time: 5 minutes | Serves 4

2 cups frozen sliced strawberries

4 kiwis, peeled and cut into

1-inch pieces

¼ cup agave nectar

¼ cup water

1. In a high-speed blender, add all the ingredients and pulse until smooth. 2. Transfer the mixture into an empty Ninja CREAMi pint container. 3. Cover the container with storage lid and freeze for 24 hours. 4. After 24 hours, remove the lid from container and arrange into the Outer Bowl of Ninja CREAMi. 5. Install the Creamerizer Paddle onto the lid of Outer Bowl. 6. Then rotate the lid clockwise to lock. 7. Press Power button to turn on the unit. 8. Then press Sorbet button. 9. When the program is completed, turn the Outer Bowl and release it from the machine. 10. Transfer the sorbet into serving bowls and serve immediately.

Pomegranate Sorbet Smile

Prep time: 5 minutes | Cook time: 45 minutes | Serves 4

1 pomegranate

½ cup white sugar

1½ tablespoons freshly

squeezed lemon juice

1½ egg whites

1 cup heavy whipping cream

1. With a knife, score the pomegranate rinds lengthwise and crosswise. With the knife, carefully break open the fruit. Using the scored lines as a guide, cut the flesh into quarters with your hands. To release the seeds, hold each quarter over a big basin and beat it forcefully with a wooden spoon. 2. To release some liquid, crush the seeds in the basin with a potato masher. Continue mashing to release additional liquid after adding the sugar and lemon juice. 3. In a glass, metal, or ceramic bowl, whisk the egg whites until firm peaks form. Mash in the pomegranate mixture. 4. In a cold glass or metal bowl, beat the cream until thick. To get the correct consistency, mash it into the pomegranate mixture, popping the seeds as needed. 5. Put the mixture into the ninja CREAMi Pint container and freeze on a level surface in a cold freezer for a full 24 hours. 6. After 24 hours, remove the Pint from the freezer. Remove the lid. 7. Place the Ninja CREAMi Pint into the outer bowl. Place the outer bowl with the Pint in it into the ninja CREAMi machine and turn until the outer bowl locks into place. Push the SORBET button. During the SORBET function, the sorbet will mix together and become very creamy. This should take approximately 2 minutes. 8. Once the SORBET function has ended, turn the outer bowl and release it from the ninja CREAMi machine. 9. Your sorbet is ready to eat! Enjoy!

Mixed Berries Sorbet

Prep time: 5 minutes | Cook time: 5 minutes | Serves 4

1 cup blueberries

1 cup raspberries

1 cup strawberries, hulled and quartered

1. In an empty Ninja CREAMi pint container, place the berries and with a potato masher, mash until well combined. 2. Cover the container with storage lid and freeze for 24 hours. 3. After 24 hours, remove the lid from container and arrange into the outer bowl of Ninja CREAMi. 4. Install the Creamerizer Paddle onto the lid of Outer Bowl. 5. Then rotate the lid clockwise to lock. 6. Press Power button to turn on the unit. 7. Then press Sorbet button. 8. When the program is completed, turn the Outer Bowl and release it from the machine. 9. Transfer the sorbet into serving bowls and serve immediately.

Pineapple Sorbet

Prep time: 5 minutes | Cook time: 5 minutes | Serves 1

12 ounces canned pineapple

1. Pour the pineapple, with the liquid from the can, into a ninja CREAMi Pint container and freeze on a level surface in a cold freezer for a full 24 hours. 2. After 24 hours, remove the Pint from the freezer. Remove the lid. 3. Place the Ninja CREAMi Pint into the outer bowl. Place the outer bowl with the Pint in it into the ninja CREAMi machine and turn until the outer bowl locks into place. Push the SORBET button. During the SORBET function, the sorbet will mix together and become very creamy. This should take approximately 2 minutes. 4. Once the SORBET function has ended, turn the outer bowl and release it from the ninja CREAMi machine. 5. Your sorbet is ready to eat! Enjoy!

Strawberry & Beet Sorbet

Prep time: 5 minutes | Cook time: 5 minutes | Serves 4

2⅔ cups strawberries, hulled and quartered

⅓ cup cooked beets, quartered

⅓ cup granulated sugar

⅓ cup orange juice

1. In a high-speed blender, add mangoes and beets and pulse until smooth. 2. Through a fine-mesh strainer, strain the mango puree into a large bowl. 3. Add the sugar and orange juice and and stir to combine. 4. Transfer the mixture into an empty Ninja CREAMi pint container. 5. Cover the container with the storage lid and freeze for 24 hours. 6. After 24 hours, remove the lid from container and arrange into the outer bowl of Ninja CREAMi. 7. Install the "Creamerizer Paddle" onto the lid of outer bowl. 8. Then rotate the lid clockwise to lock. 9. Press "Power" button to turn on the unit. 10. Then press "SORBET" button. 11. When the program is completed, turn the outer bowl and release it from the machine. 12. Transfer the sorbet into serving bowls and serve immediately.

Strawberry Sorbet

Prep time: 5 minutes | Cook time: 5 minutes | Serves 4

6 ounces daiquiri mix

2 ounces rum

½ cup frozen strawberries

½ cup simple syrup

1. In an empty Ninja CREAMi pint container, add all the ingredients and mix well. 2. Cover the container with storage lid and freeze for 24 hours. 3. After 24 hours, remove the lid from container and arrange into the Outer Bowl of Ninja CREAMi. 4. Install the Creamerizer Paddle onto the lid of Outer Bowl. 5. Then rotate the lid clockwise to lock. 6. Press Power button to turn on the unit. 7. Then press Sorbet button. 8. When the program is completed, turn the Outer Bowl and release it from the machine. 9. Transfer the sorbet into serving bowls and serve immediately.

Strawberries & Champagne Sorbet

Prep time: 5 minutes | Cook time: 15 minutes | Serves 3

1 packet strawberry-flavored gelatin (such as Jell-O)

¾ cup boiling water

½ cup light corn syrup

3 fluid ounces champagne

1 egg whites, slightly beaten

1. Dissolve the gelatin in boiling water in a bowl. Beat in the corn syrup, champagne, and egg whites. 2. Put the mixture into the ninja CREAMi Pint container and freeze on a level surface in a cold freezer for a full 24 hours. 3. After 24 hours, remove the Pint from the freezer. Remove the lid. 4. Place the Ninja CREAMi Pint into the outer bowl. Place the outer bowl with the Pint in it into the ninja CREAMi machine and turn until the outer bowl locks into

place. Push the SORBET button. During the SORBET function, the sorbet will mix together and become very creamy. This should take approximately 2 minutes. 5. Once the SORBET function has ended, turn the outer bowl and release it from the ninja CREAMi machine. 6. Your sorbet is ready to eat! Enjoy!

Mango Margarita Sorbet

Prep time: 5 minutes | Cook time: 5 minutes | Serves 4

¾ cup margarita mix

3 tablespoons gold tequila

2 tablespoons fresh lime juice

1 tablespoon agave nectar

¼ teaspoon cayenne pepper

¼ teaspoon salt

1 can mango chunks

1. In a bowl, add all ingredients except for mango chunks and beat until well combined. 2. Add mango chunks and toss to coat. 3. Transfer the mixture into an empty Ninja CREAMi pint container. 4. Cover the container with the storage lid and freeze for 24 hours. 5. After 24 hours, remove the lid from container and arrange into the outer bowl of Ninja CREAMi. 6. Install the "Creamerizer Paddle" onto the lid of outer bowl. 7. Then rotate the lid clockwise to lock. 8. Press "Power" button to turn on the unit. 9. Then press "SORBET" button. 10. When the program is completed, turn the outer bowl and release it from the machine. 11. Transfer the sorbet into serving bowls and serve immediately.

Mojito Sorbet

Prep time: 5 minutes | Cook time: 5 minutes | Serves 8

½ cup water

½ cup white sugar

¼ cup mint leaves, packed

1 teaspoon grated lime zest

½ cup freshly squeezed lime

juice

¾ cup citrus-flavored sparkling water

1 tablespoon rum (optional)

1. Add all ingredients to a bowl and mix until the sugar is dissolved. Pour into the ninja CREAMi Pint container and freeze on a level surface in a cold freezer for a full 24 hours. 2. After 24 hours, remove the Pint from the freezer. Remove the lid. 3. Place the Ninja CREAMi Pint into the outer bowl. Place the outer bowl with the Pint in it into the ninja CREAMi machine and turn until the outer bowl locks into place. Push the SORBET button. During the SORBET function, the sorbet will mix together and become very creamy. This should take approximately 2 minutes. 4. Once the SORBET function has ended, turn the outer bowl and release it from the ninja CREAMi machine. 5. Your sorbet is ready to eat! Enjoy!

Chapter 6 Milkshake Recipes

Chapter 6 Milkshake Recipes

Dairy-free Strawberry Milkshake

Prep time: 5 minutes | Cook time: 3 minutes | Serves 2

1½ cups Coconut-Vanilla Ice Cream	½ cup oat milk
	3 fresh strawberries

1. Combine the ice cream, oat milk, and strawberries in a clean CREAMi Pint. 2. Place the pint in the outer bowl of your Ninja CREAMi, install the Creamerizer Paddle in the outer bowl lid, and lock the lid assembly onto the outer bowl. Place the bowl assembly on the motor base, and twist the handle to the right to raise the platform and lock it in place. Select the Milkshake function. 3. Once the machine has finished processing, remove the milkshake from the pint. Serve immediately.

Baileys Milkshake

Prep time: 5 minutes | Cook time: 5 minutes | Serves 1

1 scoop vanilla ice cream	2 fluid ounces Baileys Irish Cream
1 scoop chocolate ice cream	
1 tablespoon chocolate sauce	1 cup whole milk
1 tablespoon caramel sauce	

1. Place all ingredients into an empty CREAMi Pint. 2. Place Pint in outer bowl, install Creamerizer Paddle onto outer bowl lid and lock the lid assembly on the outer bowl. Place the bowl assembly on the motor base and crank the lever to elevate and secure the platform in place. 3. Choose the MILKSHAKE option. 4. Remove the milkshake from the Pint after the processing is finished.

Chocolate-hazelnut Milkshake

Prep time: 5 minutes | Cook time: 3 minutes | Serves 4

2 tablespoons granulated sugar	½ cup whole milk
2 tablespoons unsweetened cocoa powder	1 cup hazelnut-flavored coffee creamer

1. In a large bowl, whisk together the sugar, cocoa powder, milk, and coffee creamer until the sugar is fully dissolved. 2. Pour the base into a clean CREAMi Pint. Place the storage lid on the container and freeze for 24 hours. 3. Remove the pint from the freezer and take off the lid. Place the pint in the outer bowl of your Ninja CREAMi, install the Creamerizer Paddle in the outer bowl lid, and lock the lid assembly onto the outer bowl. Place the bowl assembly on the motor base, and twist the handle to the right to raise the platform and lock it in place. Select the Milkshake function. 4. Once the machine has finished processing, remove the milkshake from the pint. Serve immediately.

Sugar Cookie Milkshake

Prep time: 8 minutes | Cook time: 5 minutes | Serves 1

½ cup vanilla ice cream	3 small sugar cookies, crushed
½ cup oat milk	2 tablespoons sprinkles

1. In an empty Ninja CREAMi pint container, place the ice cream. 2. With a spoon, create a 1½-inch wide hole in the center that reaches the bottom of the pint container. 3. Add the remaining ingredients into the hole. 4. Arrange the container into the outer bowl of Ninja CREAMi. 5. Install the "Creamerizer Paddle" onto the lid of outer bowl. 6. Then rotate the lid clockwise to lock. 7. Press "Power" button to turn on the unit. 8. Then press "MILKSHAKE" button. 9. When the program is completed, turn the outer bowl and release it from the machine. 10. Transfer the shake into a serving glass and serve immediately.

Boozy Amaretto Cookie Milkshake

Prep time: 5 minutes | Cook time: 3 minutes | Serves 4

1 cup whole milk	1 tablespoon agave nectar
½ cup amaretto-flavored coffee creamer	¼ cup chopped chocolate chip cookies
¼ cup amaretto liqueur	

1. In a clean CREAMi Pint, combine the milk, coffee creamer, amaretto liqueur, and agave. Stir well. Place the storage lid on the container and freeze for 24 hours. 2. Remove the pint from the freezer and take off the lid. Add the chocolate chip cookies to the top of the pint. Place the pint in the outer bowl of your Ninja CREAMi, install the Creamerizer Paddle in the outer bowl lid, and lock the lid assembly onto the outer bowl. Place the bowl assembly on the motor base, and twist the handle to the right to raise the platform and lock it in place. Select the Milkshake function. 3. Once the machine has finished processing, remove the lid. With a spoon, create a 1½-inch-wide hole that reaches the bottom of the pint. During this process, it is okay if your treat reaches above the Max Fill line. Add the chopped cookies to the hole in the pint, replace the lid, and select Milkshake. Serve immediately.

Chocolate Hazelnut Milkshake

Prep time: 6 minutes | Cook time: 10 minutes | Serves 2

1 cup chocolate ice cream
½ cup whole milk
¼ cup hazelnut spread

1. Place the ice cream in an empty CREAMi Pint. 2. Create a 1½-inch-wide hole in the bottom of the Pint using a spoon. Fill the hole with the remaining ingredients. 3. Place Pint in outer bowl, install Creamerizer Paddle onto outer bowl lid and lock the lid assembly on the outer bowl. Place bowl assembly on motor base and twist the handle right to raise the platform and lock in place. 4. Select MILKSHAKE. 5. When the milkshake has finished processing, take it from the Pint and serve right away.

Vanilla Milkshake

Prep time: 5 minutes | Cook time: 3 minutes | Serves 2

2 cups French vanilla coffee creamer
1 tablespoon agave nectar
2 ounces vodka
1 tablespoon rainbow sprinkles

1. In an empty Ninja CREAMi pint container, place all ingredients and mix well. 2. Cover the container with storage lid and freeze for 24 hours. 3. After 24 hours, remove the lid from container and arrange into the Outer Bowl of Ninja CREAMi. 4. Install the Creamerizer Paddle onto the lid of Outer Bowl. 5. Then rotate the lid clockwise to lock. 6. Press Power button to turn on the unit. 7. Then press Milkshake button. 8. When the program is completed, turn the Outer Bowl and release it from the machine. 9. Transfer the shake into serving glasses and serve immediately.

Frozen Mudslide

Prep time: 5 minutes | Cook time: 3 minutes | Serves 2

2 cups ice cubes
½ cup store-bought vanilla ice cream
6 tablespoons espresso vodka
6 tablespoons coffee-flavored liqueur
6 tablespoons Irish cream–flavored liqueur

1. Combine the ice, ice cream, vodka, and liqueurs in a blender. Blend on high until smooth. 2. Pour the base into a clean CREAMi Pint. Place the storage lid on the container and freeze for 24 hours. 3. Remove the pint from the freezer and take off the lid. Place the pint in the outer bowl of your Ninja CREAMi, install the Creamerizer Paddle in the outer bowl lid, and lock the lid assembly onto the outer bowl. Place the bowl assembly on the motor base, and twist the handle to the right to raise the platform and lock it in place. Select the Milkshake function. 4. Once the machine has finished processing, remove the milkshake from the pint. Serve immediately.

Lemon Cookie Milkshake

Prep time: 8 minutes | Cook time: 3 minutes | Serves 2

1½ cups vanilla ice cream
3 lemon cream sandwich
cookies
¼ cup milk

1. In an empty Ninja CREAMi pint container, place ice cream followed by cookies and milk. 2. Arrange the container into the Outer Bowl of Ninja CREAMi. 3. Install the Creamerizer Paddle onto the lid of Outer Bowl. 4. Then rotate the lid clockwise to lock. 5. Press Power button to turn on the unit. 6. Then press Milkshake button. 7. When the program is completed, turn the Outer Bowl and release it from the machine. 8. Transfer the shake into serving glasses and serve immediately.

Mixed Berries Milkshake

Prep time: 5 minutes | Cook time: 3 minutes | Serves 2

1½ cups vanilla ice cream
½ cup milk
½ cup fresh mixed berries

1. In an empty Ninja CREAMi pint container, place ice cream followed by milk and berries. 2. Arrange the container into the outer bowl of Ninja CREAMi. 3. Install the Creamerizer Paddle onto the lid of Outer Bowl. 4. Then rotate the lid clockwise to lock. 5. Press Power button to turn on the unit. 6. Then press Milkshake button. 7. When the program is completed, turn the Outer Bowl and release it from the machine. 8. Transfer the shake into serving glasses and serve immediately.

Lite Raspberry Ice Cream

Prep time: 5 minutes | Cook time: 3 minutes | Serves 4

1½ cups fresh raspberries
1 teaspoon freshly squeezed lemon juice
¼ cup stevia–cane sugar
sweetener blend
1 teaspoon raw agave nectar
1 cup heavy cream

1. In a blender, combine the raspberries and lemon juice; puree until smooth. 2. Pour the raspberry and lemon mixture into a large bowl, add the stevia blend and agave nectar, and mix until well combined. Stir in the heavy cream. 3. Pour the base into a clean CREAMi Pint. Place the storage lid on the container and freeze for 24 hours. 4. Remove the pint from the freezer and take off the lid. Place the pint in the outer bowl of your Ninja CREAMi, install the Creamerizer Paddle in the outer bowl lid, and lock the lid assembly onto the outer bowl. Place the bowl assembly on the motor base, and twist the handle to the right to raise the platform and lock it in place. Select the Lite Ice Cream function. 5. Once the machine has finished processing, remove the ice cream from the pint. Serve immediately.

Coffee Vodka Milkshake

Prep time: 5 minutes | Cook time: 3 minutes | Serves 2

2 cups vanilla ice cream
2 tablespoons coffee liqueur

2 tablespoons vodka

1. In an empty Ninja CREAMi pint container, place ice cream, followed by coffee liqueur and vodka. 2. Arrange the container into the outer bowl of Ninja CREAMi. 3. Install the "Creamerizer Paddle" onto the lid of outer bowl. 4. Then rotate the lid clockwise to lock. 5. Press "Power" button to turn on the unit. 6. Then press "MILKSHAKE" button. 7. When the program is completed, turn the outer bowl and release it from the machine. 8. Transfer the shake into serving glasses and serve immediately.

Marshmallow Milkshake

Prep time: 5 minutes | Cook time: 3 minutes | Serves 2

1½ cups vanilla ice cream
½ cup oat milk

½ cup marshmallow cereal

1. In an empty Ninja CREAMi pint container, place ice cream followed by oat milk and marshmallow cereal. 2. Arrange the container into the Outer Bowl of Ninja CREAMi. 3. Install the Creamerizer Paddle onto the lid of Outer Bowl. 4. Then rotate the lid clockwise to lock. 5. Press Power button to turn on the unit. 6. Then press Milkshake button. 7. When the program is completed, turn the Outer Bowl and release it from the machine. 8. Transfer the shake into serving glasses and serve immediately.

Amaretto Cookies Milkshake

Prep time: 5 minutes | Cook time: 3 minutes | Serves 2

1 cup whole milk
½ cup amaretto-flavored coffee creamer
¼ cup amaretto liqueur

1 tablespoon agave nectar
¼ cup chocolate chip cookies, chopped

1. In an empty Ninja CREAMi pint container, place all ingredients except for cookies and stir to combine. 2. Cover the container with the storage lid and freeze for 24 hours. 3. After 24 hours, remove the lid from container and arrange into the outer bowl of Ninja CREAMi. 4. Install the "Creamerizer Paddle" onto the lid of outer bowl. 5. Then rotate the lid clockwise to lock. 6. Press "Power" button to turn on the unit. 7. Then press "MILKSHAKE" button. 8. When the program is completed, with a spoon, create a 1½-inch wide hole in the center that reaches the bottom of the pint container. 9. Add the chopped cookies into the hole and press "MIX-IN" button. 10. When the program is completed, turn the outer bowl and release it from the machine. 11. Transfer the shake into serving glasses and serve immediately.

Chocolate Ginger Milkshake

Prep time: 5 minutes | Cook time: 3 minutes | Serves 2

1½ cups chocolate ice cream
½ cup oat milk

1 teaspoon ground ginger
¼ cup chocolate, grated

1. In an empty Ninja CREAMi pint container, place the ice cream. 2. With a spoon, create a 1½-inch wide hole in the center that reaches the bottom of the pint container. 3. Add the remaining ingredients into the hole. 4. Arrange the container into the outer bowl of Ninja CREAMi. 5. Install the "Creamerizer Paddle" onto the lid of outer bowl. 6. Then rotate the lid clockwise to lock. 7. Press "Power" button to turn on the unit. 8. Then press "MILKSHAKE" button. 9. When the program is completed, turn the outer bowl and release it from the machine. 10. Transfer the shake into serving glasses and serve immediately.

Mocha Tahini Milkshake

Prep time: 5 minutes | Cook time: 3 minutes | Serves 2

1½ cups chocolate ice cream
½ cup unsweetened oat milk
¼ cup tahini

2 tablespoons coffee
1 tablespoon chocolate fudge

1. In an empty Ninja CREAMi pint container, place ice cream followed by milk, tahini, coffee and fudge. 2. Arrange the container into the Outer Bowl of Ninja CREAMi. 3. Install the Creamerizer Paddle onto the lid of Outer Bowl. 4. Then rotate the lid clockwise to lock. 5. Press Power button to turn on the unit. 6. Then press Milkshake button. 7. When the program is completed, turn the Outer Bowl and release it from the machine. 8. Transfer the shake into serving glasses and serve immediately.

Avocado Milkshake

Prep time: 5 minutes | Cook time: 5 minutes | Serves 2

1 cup coconut ice cream
1 small ripe avocado, peeled, pitted and chopped
1 teaspoon fresh lemon juice

2 tablespoons agave nectar
1 teaspoon vanilla extract
Pinch of salt
½ cup oat milk

1. In an empty Ninja CREAMi pint container, place ice cream, followed by remaining ingredients. 2. Arrange the container into the outer bowl of Ninja CREAMi. 3. Install the "Creamerizer Paddle" onto the lid of outer bowl. 4. Then rotate the lid clockwise to lock. 5. Press "Power" button to turn on the unit. 6. Then press "MILKSHAKE" button. 7. When the program is completed, turn the outer bowl and release it from the machine. 8. Transfer the shake into serving glasses and serve immediately.

Banana Milkshake

Prep time: 5 minutes | Cook time: 3 minutes | Serves 2

1 scoop vanilla ice cream
2 small bananas, peeled and halved

7 fluid ounces semi-skimmed milk

1. In an empty Ninja CREAMi pint container, place ice cream followed by bananas and milk. 2. Arrange the container into the Outer Bowl of Ninja CREAMi. 3. Install the Creamerizer Paddle onto the lid of Outer Bowl. 4. Then rotate the lid clockwise to lock. 5. Press Power button to turn on the unit. 6. Then press Milkshake button. 7. When the program is completed, turn the Outer Bowl and release it from the machine. 8. Transfer the shake into serving glasses and serve immediately.

Lite Peanut Butter Ice Cream

Prep time: 5 minutes | Cook time: 3 minutes | Serves 4

1¾ cups fat-free (skim) milk
¼ cup stevia–cane sugar blend
1 teaspoon vanilla extract

3 tablespoons smooth peanut butter

1. In a medium bowl, whisk together the milk, stevia blend, vanilla extract, and peanut butter until the mixture is smooth and the stevia is fully dissolved. Let the mixture sit for about 5 minutes, until any foam subsides. If the stevia is still not dissolved, whisk again. 2. Pour the base into a clean CREAMi Pint. Place the storage lid on the container and freeze for 24 hours. 3. Remove the pint from the freezer and take off the lid. Place the pint in the outer bowl of your Ninja CREAMi, install the Creamerizer Paddle in the outer bowl lid, and lock the lid assembly onto the outer bowl. Place the bowl assembly on the motor base, and twist the handle to the right to raise the platform and lock it in place. Select the Lite Ice Cream function. 4. Once the machine has finished processing, remove the ice cream from the pint. Serve immediately.

Healthy Strawberry Shake

Prep time: 5 minutes | Cook time: 10 minutes | Serves 1

1 cup milk
1 tablespoon honey

½ teaspoon vanilla extract
½ cup frozen strawberries

1. Add the milk, honey, vanilla extract, and strawberries into an empty CREAMi Pint. 2. Place Pint in outer bowl, install Creamerizer Paddle onto outer bowl lid and lock the lid assembly on the outer bowl. Place the bowl assembly on the motor base and crank the lever to elevate and secure the platform in place. 3. Select MILKSHAKE. 4. Remove the milkshake from the Pint after the processing is finished.

Caramel Cone Milkshake

Prep time: 5 minutes | Cook time: 3 minutes | Serves 4

1½ cups vanilla ice cream
½ cup whole milk
3 tablespoons caramel sauce

1 waffle cone, crushed or finely chopped

1. Combine the vanilla ice cream, milk, and caramel sauce in a clean CREAMi Pint. 2. With a spoon, create a 1½-inch-wide hole that reaches the bottom of the pint. During this process, it is okay if your treat reaches above the Max Fill line. Add the crushed waffle cone to the hole in the pint. 3. Place the pint in the outer bowl of your Ninja CREAMi, install the Creamerizer Paddle in the outer bowl lid, and lock the lid assembly onto the outer bowl. Place the bowl assembly on the motor base, and twist the handle to the right to raise the platform and lock it in place. Select the Milkshake function. 4. Once the machine has finished processing, remove the milkshake from the pint. Serve immediately.

Mocha Milkshake

Prep time: 5 minutes | Cook time: 3 minutes | Serves 2

1½ cups chocolate ice cream
½ cup cashew milk
½ cup ripe banana, peeled and

cut into ½-inch pieces
1 tablespoon instant coffee powder

1. In an empty Ninja CREAMi pint container, place ice cream followed by milk, banana and coffee powder. 2. Arrange the container into the Outer Bowl of Ninja CREAMi. 3. Install the Creamerizer Paddle onto the lid of Outer Bowl. 4. Then rotate the lid clockwise to lock. 5. Press Power button to turn on the unit. 6. Then press Milkshake button. 7. When the program is completed, turn the Outer Bowl and release it from the machine. 8. Transfer the shake into serving glasses and serve immediately.

Peanut Butter And Jelly Milkshake

Prep time: 5 minutes | Cook time: 5 minutes | Serves 2

3 tablespoons peanut butter
3 tablespoons grape jelly
1 cup milk

5 ice cubes
½ teaspoon vanilla extract

1. Add the milk, peanut butter, ice cubes, vanilla extract, and grape jelly into an empty CREAMi Pint. 2. Place the Pint in the outer bowl, install the Creamerizer Paddle onto the outer bowl lid and lock the lid assembly on the outer bowl. Place the bowl assembly on the motor base and crank the lever to elevate and secure the platform in place. 3. Choose the MILKSHAKE option. 4. Remove the milkshake from the Pint after the processing is finished.

Cacao Matcha Milkshake

Prep time: 5 minutes | Cook time: 3 minutes | Serves 2

1½ cups vanilla ice cream
½ cup canned full-fat coconut milk
1 teaspoon matcha powder

¼ cup cacao nibs
¾ teaspoon peppermint extract
¼ teaspoon vanilla extract

1. In an empty Ninja CREAMi pint container, place ice cream, followed by coconut milk, matcha powder, cacao nibs and peppermint extract. 2. Arrange the container into the outer bowl of Ninja CREAMi. 3. Install the "Creamerizer Paddle" onto the lid of outer bowl. 4. Then rotate the lid clockwise to lock. 5. Press "Power" button to turn on the unit. 6. Then press "MILKSHAKE" button. 7. When the program is completed, turn the outer bowl and release it from the machine. 8. Transfer the shake into serving glasses and serve immediately.

Pecan Milkshake

Prep time: 5 minutes | Cook time: 3 minutes | Serves 2

1½ cups vanilla ice cream
½ cup unsweetened soy milk
2 tablespoons maple syrup

¼ cup pecans, chopped
1 teaspoon ground cinnamon
Pinch of salt

1. In an empty Ninja CREAMi pint container, place ice cream followed by soy milk, maple syrup, pecans, cinnamon and salt. 2. Arrange the container into the Outer Bowl of Ninja CREAMi. 3. Install the Creamerizer Paddle onto the lid of Outer Bowl. 4. Then rotate the lid clockwise to lock. 5. Press Power button to turn on the unit. 6. Then press Milkshake button. 7. When the program is completed, turn the Outer Bowl and release it from the machine. 8. Transfer the shake into serving glasses and serve immediately.

Lemon Meringue Pie Milkshake

Prep time: 5 minutes | Cook time: 5 minutes | Serves 1

1 cup vanilla ice cream
4 tablespoons store-bought lemon curd, divided
4 tablespoons marshmallow

topping, divided
½ cup Graham Crackers, broken, divided

1. Place the ice cream in an empty CREAMi Pint. 2. Use a spoon to create a 1½-inch wide hole that reaches the bottom of the Pint. Add the remaining ingredients to the hole. 3. Place Pint in outer bowl, install Creamerizer Paddle onto outer bowl lid and lock the lid assembly on the outer bowl. Place the bowl assembly on the motor base and crank the lever to elevate and secure the platform in place. 4. Select the MILKSHAKE option. 5. Remove the milkshake from the Pint after the processing is finished.

Chocolate-peanut Butter Milkshake

Prep time: 5 minutes | Cook time: 3 minutes | Serves 2

1½ cups chocolate ice cream
½ cup whole milk

¼ cup mini peanut butter cups

1. Combine the chocolate ice cream and milk in a clean CREAMi Pint. 2. Use a spoon to create a 1½-inch-wide hole that goes all the way to the bottom of the pint. Pour the mini peanut butter cups into the hole. 3. Place the pint in the outer bowl of your Ninja CREAMi, install the Creamerizer Paddle in the outer bowl lid, and lock the lid assembly onto the outer bowl. Place the bowl assembly on the motor base, and twist the handle to the right to raise the platform and lock it in place. Select the Milkshake function. 4. Once the machine has finished processing, remove the milkshake from the pint. Serve immediately.

Lime Sherbet Milkshake

Prep time: 5 minutes | Cook time: 3 minutes | Serves 1

1½ cups rainbow sherbet

½ cup lime seltzer

1. In an empty Ninja CREAMi pint container, place sherbet and top with lime seltzer. 2. Arrange the container into the outer bowl of Ninja CREAMi. 3. Install the "Creamerizer Paddle" onto the lid of outer bowl. 4. Then rotate the lid clockwise to lock. 5. Press "Power" button to turn on the unit. 6. Then press "MILKSHAKE" button. 7. When the program is completed, turn the outer bowl and release it from the machine. 8. Transfer the shake into a serving glass and serve immediately.

Peanut Butter Brownie Milkshake

Prep time: 5 minutes | Cook time: 5 minutes | Serves 2

½ cup chocolate ice cream
½ cup whole milk
2 tablespoons peanut butter, for mix-in

1¼ cups brownies, chopped into bite-sized pieces, for mix-in

1. Place the ice cream in an empty CREAMi Pint. 2. Use a spoon to create a 1½-inch wide hole that reaches the bottom of the Pint. Add the remaining ingredients to the hole. 3. Place Pint in outer bowl, install Creamerizer Paddle onto outer bowl lid and lock the lid assembly on the outer bowl. Place the bowl assembly on the motor base and crank the lever to elevate and secure the platform in place. 4. Select MILKSHAKE. 5. Remove the milkshake from the Pint after the processing is finished.

Cashew Butter Milkshake

Prep time: 5 minutes | Cook time: 3 minutes | Serves 2

1½ cups vanilla ice cream
½ cup canned cashew milk

¼ cup cashew butter

1. In an empty Ninja CREAMi pint container, place the ice cream. 2. With a spoon, create a 1½-inch wide hole in the center that reaches the bottom of the pint container. 3. Add the remaining ingredients into the hole. 4. Arrange the container into the Outer Bowl of Ninja CREAMi. 5. Install the Creamerizer Paddle onto the lid of Outer Bowl. 6. Then rotate the lid clockwise to lock. 7. Press Power button to turn on the unit. 8. Then press Milkshake button. 9. When the program is completed, turn the Outer Bowl and release it from the machine. 10. Transfer the shake into serving glasses and serve immediately.

Chocolate Yogurt Milkshake

Prep time: 5 minutes | Cook time: 3 minutes | Serves 2

1 cup frozen chocolate yogurt
1 scoop chocolate whey protein

powder
1 cup whole milk

1. In an empty Ninja CREAMi pint container, place yogurt followed by protein powder and milk. 2. Arrange the container into the Outer Bowl of Ninja CREAMi. 3. Install the Creamerizer Paddle onto the lid of Outer Bowl. 4. Then rotate the lid clockwise to lock. 5. Press Power button to turn on the unit. 6. Then press Milkshake button. 7. When the program is completed, turn the Outer Bowl and release it from the machine. 8. Transfer the shake into serving glasses and serve immediately.

Lite Coffee Chip Ice Cream

Prep time: 5 minutes | Cook time: 3 minutes | Serves 4

¾ cup unsweetened coconut
cream
¼ cup monk fruit sweetener
with erythritol
½ teaspoon stevia sweetener
1½ tablespoons instant coffee

granules
1 cup unsweetened rice milk
1 teaspoon vanilla extract
¼ cup low-sugar vegan
chocolate chips

1. In a large bowl, whisk the coconut cream until smooth. Add the monk fruit sweetener, stevia, instant coffee, rice milk, and vanilla to the bowl; whisk until everything is well combined and the sugar is dissolved. 2. Pour the base into a clean CREAMi Pint. Place the storage lid on the container and freeze for 24 hours. 3. Remove the pint from the freezer and take off the lid. Place the pint in the outer bowl of your Ninja CREAMi, install the Creamerizer Paddle in the outer bowl lid, and lock the lid assembly onto the outer bowl. Place the bowl assembly on the motor base, and twist the handle to the right to raise the platform and lock it in place. Select the Lite Ice Cream function. 4. Use a spoon to create a 1½-inch-wide hole that goes all the way to the bottom of the pint. Pour the chocolate chips into the hole. then replace the pint lid and select the Mix-In function. 5. Once the machine has finished processing, remove the ice cream from the pint. Serve immediately.

Chocolate Liqueur Milkshake

Prep time: 5 minutes | Cook time: 3 minutes | Serves 2

2 cups vanilla ice cream
⅓ cup chocolate liqueur

⅓ cup whole milk

1. In an empty Ninja CREAMi pint container, place ice cream, followed by chocolate liqueur and milk. 2. Arrange the container into the outer bowl of Ninja CREAMi. 3. Install the "Creamerizer Paddle" onto the lid of outer bowl. 4. Then rotate the lid clockwise to lock. 5. Press "Power" button to turn on the unit. 6. Then press "MILKSHAKE" button. 7. When the program is completed, turn the outer bowl and release it from the machine. 8. Transfer the shake into serving glasses and serve immediately.

Chocolate Ice Cream Milkshake

Prep time: 5 minutes | Cook time: 3 minutes | Serves 1

1½ cups chocolate ice cream

½ cup whole milk

1. In an empty Ninja CREAMi pint container, place ice cream, followed by milk. 2. Arrange the container into the Outer Bowl of Ninja CREAMi. 3. Install the Creamerizer Paddle onto the lid of Outer Bowl. 4. Then rotate the lid clockwise to lock. 5. Press Power button to turn on the unit. 6. Then press Milkshake button. 7. When the program is completed, turn the Outer Bowl and release it from the machine. 8. Transfer the shake into a serving glass and serve immediately.

Dulce De Leche Milkshake

Prep time: 5 minutes | Cook time: 5 minutes | Serves 2

1 cup vanilla or coffee ice
cream
½ cup milk

2 tablespoons sweetened
condensed milk
¼ teaspoon salt

1. Place all ingredients into an empty CREAMi Pint. 2. Place Pint in outer bowl, install Creamerizer Paddle onto outer bowl lid and lock the lid assembly on the outer bowl. Place the bowl assembly on the motor base and crank the lever to elevate and secure the platform in place. 3. Choose the MILKSHAKE option. 4. Remove the milkshake from the Pint after the function is finished.

Cacao Mint Milkshake

Prep time: 5 minutes | Cook time: 3 minutes | Serves 2

1½ cups vanilla ice cream
½ cup canned full-fat coconut milk
1 teaspoon matcha powder

¼ cup cacao nibs
1 teaspoon peppermint extract

1. In an empty Ninja CREAMi pint container, place ice cream followed by coconut milk, matcha powder, cacao nibs and peppermint extract. 2. Arrange the container into the Outer Bowl of Ninja CREAMi. 3. Install the Creamerizer Paddle onto the lid of Outer Bowl. 4. Then rotate the lid clockwise to lock. 5. Press Power button to turn on the unit. 6. Then press Milkshake button. 7. When the program is completed, turn the Outer Bowl and release it from the machine. 8. Transfer the shake into serving glasses and serve immediately.

Appendix 1: Measurement Conversion Chart

MEASUREMENT CONVERSION CHART

VOLUME EQUIVALENTS(DRY)

US STANDARD	METRIC (APPROXIMATE)
1/8 teaspoon	0.5 mL
1/4 teaspoon	1 mL
1/2 teaspoon	2 mL
3/4 teaspoon	4 mL
1 teaspoon	5 mL
1 tablespoon	15 mL
1/4 cup	59 mL
1/2 cup	118 mL
3/4 cup	177 mL
1 cup	235 mL
2 cups	475 mL
3 cups	700 mL
4 cups	1 L

VOLUME EQUIVALENTS(LIQUID)

US STANDARD	US STANDARD (OUNCES)	METRIC (APPROXIMATE)
2 tablespoons	1 fl.oz.	30 mL
1/4 cup	2 fl.oz.	60 mL
1/2 cup	4 fl.oz.	120 mL
1 cup	8 fl.oz.	240 mL
1 1/2 cup	12 fl.oz.	355 mL
2 cups or 1 pint	16 fl.oz.	475 mL
4 cups or 1 quart	32 fl.oz.	1 L
1 gallon	128 fl.oz.	4 L

TEMPERATURES EQUIVALENTS

FAHRENHEIT(F)	CELSIUS(C) (APPROXIMATE)
225 °F	107 °C
250 °F	120 °C
275 °F	135 °C
300 °F	150 °C
325 °F	160 °C
350 °F	180 °C
375 °F	190 °C
400 °F	205 °C
425 °F	220 °C
450 °F	235 °C
475 °F	245 °C
500 °F	260 °C

WEIGHT EQUIVALENTS

US STANDARD	METRIC (APPROXIMATE)
1 ounce	28 g
2 ounces	57 g
5 ounces	142 g
10 ounces	284 g
15 ounces	425 g
16 ounces (1 pound)	455 g
1.5 pounds	680 g
2 pounds	907 g

Made in the USA
Monee, IL
31 May 2023

35043072R00033